Product-Risk Labeling

AEI STUDIES IN REGULATION AND FEDERALISM
Christopher C. DeMuth and Jonathan R. Macey, series editors

FEDERALISM IN TAXATION: THE CASE FOR GREATER UNIFORMITY
Daniel Shaviro

PRODUCT-RISK LABELING: A FEDERAL RESPONSIBILITY
W. Kip Viscusi

STATE AND FEDERAL REGULATION OF NATIONAL ADVERTISING
J. Howard Beales and Timothy J. Muris

COSTLY POLICIES: STATE REGULATION AND ANTITRUST EXEMPTION IN
INSURANCE MARKETS
Jonathan R. Macey and Geoffrey P. Miller

Product-Risk Labeling

A Federal Responsibility

W. Kip Viscusi

The AEI Press

Publisher for the American Enterprise Institute
WASHINGTON, D.C.

1993

Distributed to the Trade by National Book Network, 15200 NBN Way, Blue Ridge Summit, PA 17214. To order call toll free 1-800-462-6420 or 1-717-794-3800. For all other inquiries please contact the AEI Press, 1150 Seventeenth Street, N.W., Washington, D.C. 20036 or call 1-800-862-5801.

Library of Congress Cataloging-in-Publication Data

Viscusi, W. Kip.
    Product-risk labeling : a federal responsibility / W. Kip Viscusi.
      p.   cm.
    ISBN 0-8447-3821-2. — ISBN 0-8447-3820-4 (pbk.)
    1. Labels—Law and legislation—California—Compliance costs.
  2. Consumer goods—Labeling—Economic aspects—United States.
  3. Risk communication—Economic aspects—United States.   I. Title.
HF5773.L3V57   1992
658.5′64—dc20   92-35079
                                                      CIP

1 3 5 7 9 10 8 6 4 2

THE AEI PRESS
Publisher for the American Enterprise Institute
1150 17th Street, N.W., Washington, D.C. 20036

Contents

CONTENTS

Foreword

W. KIP VISCUSI'S STUDY of state and federal regulation of product labeling is one of a series of research monographs commissioned by the American Enterprise Institute's Regulation and Federalism Project. The purpose of the project is to examine the advantages and disadvantages of American federalism in important areas of contemporary business regulation, including advertising, insurance, transportation, taxation, communications, and environmental quality.

The benefits of state autonomy—diversity, responsiveness to local circumstances, and constraint on the power of the national government—are fundamental to the American political creed and deeply embedded in our political institutions. Are these benefits real and substantial in the case of business regulation? How do they compare with the costs of duplication, inconsistency, and interference with free interstate commerce that state regulation can entail? Has the growth of national and international commerce altered the balance of federalism's benefits and costs—for example, by affecting the ability of individual states to pursue local policies at the expense of citizens of other states? Are there practical means of reducing the economic costs of state autonomy in regulation while preserving its political benefits?

The authors of these volumes have found different answers to these questions in the context of different markets and regulatory regimes: they call for greater national uniformity in some cases, greater state autonomy in others, and a revision of the rules of state "policy competition" in still others. We hope that this research will be useful to officials and legislators at all levels of government and to the business executives who must live with their policies. More generally, we hope that the AEI project will prove to be a significant contribution to our understanding of one of the most distinctive and important features of American government.

FOREWORD

Each of the monographs produced for the Regulation and Federalism Project was discussed and criticized at an AEI seminar involving federal and state lawmakers, business executives, professionals, and academic experts with a wide range of interests and viewpoints. I would like to thank all of them for their contributions, noting, however, that final exposition and conclusions were entirely the work of the authors of each monograph. I am particularly grateful to Jonathan R. Macey of Cornell University and Heather Gradison of AEI, who organized and directed the project's research and seminars along with me, and to John D. Ong and Jon V. Heider of the BFGoodrich Company and Patricia H. Engman of the Business Roundtable, who suggested the project in the first place, worked hard and effectively to raise financial support for it, and provided valuable counsel and encouragement throughout.

CHRISTOPHER C. DeMUTH
President, American Enterprise Institute
for Public Policy Research

About the Author

W. Kip Viscusi is the George G. Allen Professor of Economics at Duke University, as well as director of the Program on Risk Analysis and Civil Liability. He is the author of fourteen books, including *Fatal Tradeoffs: Public & Private Responsibilities for Risk* (1992) and *Smoking: Making the Risky Decision* (1992), and of more than a hundred articles concerning risk regulation. His *Employment Hazards: An Investigation of Market Performance* won Harvard's David A. Wells Prize.

Mr. Viscusi received his A.B. summa cum laude in 1971, his master's degree in public policy in 1973, and his Ph.D. in economics in 1976, all from Harvard University. He has taught at Northwestern University and at the University of Chicago, and he has served on advisory committees for the Environmental Protection Agency since 1987. Mr. Viscusi is also a research associate for the National Bureau of Economic Research and an adjunct fellow in civil justice for the Manhattan Institute.

Illustration by Hatley Mason.
Reprinted, by permission, from *The Sacramento Bee.*

1

Hazard Warnings

HISTORICALLY, the primary responsibility for the safety and labeling of food and drug products has been with the federal government. A complex set of regulations governs which products can be marketed and what information should be provided to consumers.

Beginning in 1986 with California's Proposition 65, the states have become increasingly active in issuing regulations that will affect the labeling of food, drugs, cosmetics, and medical devices. These labeling requirements impose substantial burdens on firms, which must assess the risks associated with a product, determine whether a label is warranted, provide a label if necessary, reformulate products if they wish to avoid labeling, and defend themselves in lawsuits.

The purpose of this study is to analyze the economic ramifications of these risk-communication efforts. In particular, what will be the effect on society? There exists substantial uncertainty regarding the ultimate impact of these efforts, since the distribution and level of chemicals in food, drugs, and cosmetics is not yet known; nor do we know the compliance decisions that will be made by firms. Nevertheless, this study indicates that these efforts create substantial burdens on industry and may even prove harmful to the intended beneficiaries—consumers.

Hazard Warnings as a Regulatory Policy

Hazard warnings represent an intermediate form of government intervention. One option is for the government to regulate the risk attributes of the product directly, with the most extreme form of regulation being a product ban. At the other extreme is no regulation whatsoever. Hazard warnings lie between these extremes in that the product remains on the market in its current form, but an effort is made to alert users of the product to the risks that are posed by it.

The intent is to provide consumers with information that will enable them to undertake appropriate risk-reduction actions. These responses can be of two forms. The first is a threshold decision whether or not to purchase the product. The second is how the product will be used. The warnings policies considered in this study focus on risk information provided with respect to the purchase decision rather than on appropriate product use once the product has been acquired.

The government might choose this intermediate type of policy option for a variety of reasons. First, the government is often in a situation of uncertainty. It may not have enough information to warrant taking firm action against a product, but at least it feels a duty to provide consumers with information so that those wishing to exercise caution can do so. Such warnings efforts generally are only stopgap measures, since the government is probably better situated to make informed scientific judgments than are consumers, who are given vague exhortations to exercise caution.

The second rationale for a warnings policy is that legitimate risk-taking choices are often available to individuals. A no-risk society is neither feasible nor desirable. Moreover, individuals differ with respect to their risk preferences, so that some individuals might choose to incur risks that others find unattractive. When consumers are provided with information regarding the levels of risk, they can match the risks and benefits of the products they choose with their own preferences.

A third rationale for warnings is that in many situations the risk cannot be addressed through a centralized regulatory policy but must necessarily be reduced through decentralized actions. Precautions with regard to chemical and pesticide products offer one example. The government cannot monitor the use of these products, so instead it gives consumers instructions for mixing these chemicals and applying them. In cases of extreme risk, in which the risk of error in such decentralized actions is too great, the government can introduce additional controls—for example, requirements that only certified pesticide applicators work with particularly risky pesticides.

A final rationale for warnings is that government regulators may settle on this intermediate policy option as a compromise. If interest groups representing industry oppose stringent regulation, such as a product ban, officials may view a hazard warning as the optimal

2

achievable policy option rather than an ideal one.

The task of a hazard-warning policy is to promote informed choice. In the case of product purchase, the objective is to provide individuals with sufficient information regarding the risk so they can balance the costs imposed by the risk against the benefits they derive from the product. When judging an informational effort, the reference point should be whether it promotes individual understanding of the risks and subsequent rational decisions with respect to them.

All consumers need not understand the risk for a warning to be successful. In the case of general demand for a product and warnings associated with product purchase, it is sufficient for a core group of consumers to be knowledgeable, since the marginal consumers who are most responsive to the product's attractiveness will drive the market price. In the case of risks to particular segments of the population that must exercise care, a targeted warning directed only at that population is needed. Reproductive hazards are pertinent to pregnant women, for example, and possibly to their spouses.

Although this objective is assumed to discourage the purchase of a product, hazard warnings should not be alarmist. If discouraging purchases were the policy objective, that could be done more effectively by banning the product altogether.

As an intermediate policy option, hazard warnings do not mandate that individuals take precautions; they are not required to follow the warnings. Indeed, they are not required even to read the warnings. In efficacy, warnings have had a mixed record. Warnings that provide new and useful knowledge can lead to the desired consumer response. In contrast, warnings that do not provide new knowledge but attempt to browbeat consumers into changing their behavior have proved less successful.

Examples of the mixed performance of warnings efforts abound. A Food and Drug Administration (FDA) study of consumer awareness of salt- or sodium-content listings on consumer products found that only one-fourth of all respondents could recall them; only 40 percent could recall reading an ingredient list; and fewer than half read health-related information on food labels.[1] These findings are somewhat higher than those of an earlier study, which indicated that only

---

[1] James T. Heinbach, "The Public Responds to Labeling of the Sodium Content of Foods," Food and Drug Administration, 1983.

15 percent of all consumers compare nutrition labels and only 10 percent use nutrition-labeling information when making their purchase decisions.[2]

The performance of drug-related products is not much different. Although 88 percent of oral-contraceptive users claim to have read the patient package inserts, only 69 percent can recall dosage information and only 50 percent can recall information on common reactions to oral contraceptives.[3] One of the most commonly read warnings for a drug product is that on aspirin. In this case, one-fourth of all aspirin users are aware of the Reye's syndrome warning, 53 percent are aware of the contraindications against using aspirin in the case of flu, and 40 percent could recall that Reye's syndrome was mentioned on the label.[4]

Even when individuals note the warning information, they may not follow the advice offered. Studies of home-safety practice training programs, the "buckle up for safety" seat belt campaign, and the Consumer Product Safety Commission's "project burn prevention" indicate that these programs, which offer little new information, had little effect on safety-related behavior.[5] Canadian consumers seldom use the energy-efficiency labeling information provided them when purchasing appliances.[6] Product-safety information was also found to have little effect on the safety knowledge of students or on the safety precautions they took.[7]

In contrast, labels that provide new information to consumers

[2]R. J. Lenahan, et al., "Consumer Reaction to Nutritional Labels on Food Products," *Journal of Consumer Research*, vol. 4 (1973), pp. 119–28.

[3]Louis A. Morris, Michael B. Mazis, and Evelyn Gordon, "A Survey of the Effects of Oral Contraceptive Patient Information," *Journal of the American Medical Association*, vol. 238 (1977), pp. 2504–08.

[4]Louis A. Morris and Robert Klimberg, "A Survey of Aspirin Use and Reye's Syndrome Awareness among Parents," *American Journal of Public Health*, vol. 76 (1986), pp. 1422–24.

[5]Robert S. Adler and R. David Pittle, "Cajolery or Command: Are Education Campaigns Inadequate Substitutes for Regulation?" *Yale Journal on Regulation*, vol. 1 (1984), pp. 159–94.

[6]John Claxton and C. Dennis Anderson, "Energy Information at the Point of Sale: A Field Experiment," *Advances in Consumer Research*, vol. 17 (1980), pp. 277–82.

[7]Richard Staelin, "The Effects of Consumer Education on Consumer Product Safety Behavior," *Journal of Consumer Research*, vol. 5 (1978), pp. 30–40.

about chemical hazards can have an effect, but they will not lead to universal precaution-taking. After reading various warning labels for common household chemicals, the fraction of consumers who would undertake the precautions for bleach use ranged from 23 to 84 percent, and the group who would undertake the recommended precautions for drain opener consist of 61 to 82 percent of the sample.[8] Providing additional information can foster sounder decisions but will not ensure safer outcomes.

The advantage of informational programs is that if they do provide new knowledge to consumers, they enable the individual to make the particular risk trade-off he or she believes most appropriate, given individual preferences. Those who are highly averse to bearing risk can undertake the precaution; those who place a lower value on health risks can forgo it. Hazard warnings consequently promote an efficient matchup of risk-precautionary effort and risk-dollar trade-offs among consumers, enabling individuals to express the heterogeneity of their attitudes through their behavior. In contrast, bans of risky products eliminate this role for consumer discretion and limit the opportunities of consumers who are willing to bear risk.

To assist in this regard, the warnings effort must provide accurate information that can serve as a useful basis for correct decisions. Warnings efforts that are unduly alarmist and are designed simply to discourage product use will not achieve this objective. Consequently, any warnings program should be tested to determine how well it conveys new knowledge and accurate risk perceptions to consumers. In the text that follows, the assessment of Proposition 65 and related measures indicates that there is a legitimate role for these efforts, but they are not now designed to foster accurate perceptions to consumers or to provide a basis for efficient risk-taking decisions.

Hazard Warnings and the Federalism Debate

The rationale for state control of warnings is similar to that for other regulatory policies. If preferences vary from state to state, then the state can match the regulatory outcome and the character of hazard warnings with the preferences of its residents better than the federal

---

[8]W. Kip Viscusi and Wesley A. Magat, *Learning about Risk: Consumer and Worker Responses to Hazard Information* (Cambridge: Harvard University Press, 1987).

government can. States with residents who are particularly concerned about risks can adopt hazard warnings; other states need not.

Despite inaction by the federal government, one would not expect there to be the kinds of state differences that would lead to stronger rationales for warnings in particular states. Hazard warnings do not mandate a particular level of product safety: they simply provide information. Individuals who place a low value on risk or who already understand the risks are free to ignore this information, whereas others may be swayed by it. Because use of the information by consumers is discretionary, there is less need to match the regulatory policy to the preferences of the citizens than if, for example, a regulation were to mandate a particular safety level.

Adopting warnings in all states does not force those who are willing to bear risks to purchase safer products, as uniform product-safety standards would do. Since the most influential factor in determining willingness to bear risks is the individual's income status, and income levels within all states vary considerably, there are substantial differences in attitudes toward risk within states.

Because hazard warnings lead to decentralized decisions involving risks, they do not constrain the choices of heterogeneous decision makers in different states. Other labeling efforts are likely to have quite different characteristics. Uniform efficiency ratings for air conditioners, for example, may be difficult to provide when states such as Maine and Florida have such different weather.

The federal government has an advantage in pursuing a labeling program, particularly if it has a substantial scientific component. Reviews of the hazard-warnings efforts initiated by California and other states indicates that the states have little independent scientific knowledge for product-risk labeling. For the most part, these states have proposed that independent scientific advisory groups be formed to use the results of federal agencies' classifications of carcinogens or reproductive toxicants.

Federal regulation also offers the advantage of economies of scale. The review of the impact of state regulations indicates that distinct state-warnings efforts impose particular burdens on firms that market products nationally. The effect of diverse state warnings is to carve up a national market into a series of separate state markets, creating barriers to entry and imposing unnecessary costs.

If some intermediate policy option between product bans and no

6

regulation is feasible, then presumably it is at the federal level. There is already some precedent for federal intervention. Hazard warnings for saccharin and cigarettes are mandated by Congress. The Food and Drug Administration (FDA) regulates the hazard warnings for pharmaceutical products. The U.S. Environmental Protection Agency (EPA) controls the warnings for pesticides and chemical products. Similarly, a broad array of consumer and job-related federal regulations pertains to hazard warnings.

This does not mean that no role remains for the warnings considered in this study. These federal regulations are not comprehensive. Indeed, with the exception of the aforementioned products and such selected risky products as cigarettes, no federally mandated warnings cover food, drugs, or cosmetics. Moreover, no mechanism determines whether shoe polish or breakfast cereal should receive a warning. The state warning efforts addressed here focus on classes of risk not currently captured through federal regulatory policies. The issue is whether the role of federal regulation should be extended to consider these classes of risk, or responsibility for intermediate risks from food, drugs, cosmetics, and medical devices should be relegated to the states. The evidence supports federal involvement in this area.

Principal Findings

The main findings of this study are the following:

- The first major state warning effort was California's Proposition 65, which mandated hazard warnings for risks of cancer and reproductive toxicity from products, jobs, and the environment. This multipurpose, statewide referendum also addressed other environmental concerns. According to survey data, only a small proportion of those voting for this measure indicated that support of the hazard-warning component influenced their decision.
- Proposition 65 imposes substantial risk-communication responsibilities on firms. Firms must determine whether their products have sufficient amounts of carcinogens and reproductive toxicants to warrant labels. The threshold for this determination is a lifetime risk of 1/100,000—one case of cancer for every 100,000 product users over lifetime product use—for carcinogens. For reproductive toxicants, the cutoff is the amount for which 1,000 times the exposure will have

7

no observable effects. A bounty provision and the penalty provisions of the act provide strong financial incentives for compliance.

• Eight other states are considering or have considered Proposition 65 types of measures, and many currently have bills pending before state legislatures. Several other states have proposed limited warning efforts for BST and selected other food-and-drug products, such as ibuprofen. This proliferation of warnings efforts fragments national markets for products and creates uncertainty.

• Product coverage of these measures differs, but the most comprehensive includes food, drugs, cosmetics, medical devices, and other consumer products. Implementing the regulations for California's Proposition 65 provides a temporary exemption for products in compliance with state and federal food and drug regulations. But a California trial court has invalidated this exemption in a decision currently on appeal. Unless it is reversed, the scope of Proposition 65 will be substantially broadened to include all products within the above-mentioned categories. The California courts have upheld an exemption for naturally occurring carcinogens present in foods in unavoidable levels.

• Despite some variations in approach, other state regulations are patterned after California's Proposition 65 in risk threshold, in the nature of the warning conveyed, and in the wording of the warning. Differences across states are minor, but they are sufficient to require a firm to provide separate warnings for different states. Warnings in compliance in one state would require a different language in others. The required inclusion of the state name and minor variations would mandate distinct labeling approaches. This would divide the country not into just two groups—those with a warning and those without— but rather into one group of the states that do not impose warnings and a series of other groups, represented by each state with a warnings policy.

• The acceptable modes of compliance differ, as each state offers firms a variety of choices. On a practical basis, firms have less flexibility. In California, for example, firms selected three options from among the alternatives: advertising, a toll-free number, and an in-store sign. The industry lawsuit to determine that this method complied with Proposition 65 was unsuccessful, although it remains on appeal. In-store warnings create a variety of practical implementation problems and loss of control over the warning provision by the producing firm. Most industry experts believe that on-product labeling is the likely option for companies that choose to warn. Some states even require the industry to show that on-product labeling is infeasible before it can consider other alternatives.

• The states that have pursued the Proposition 65 type of initiative represent a substantial portion of the national market. California alone represents 15 percent of the national drug market and 12 percent of the national grocery market; New York and Ohio bring the national-market share represented to roughly one-fourth. Massachusetts and Illinois bring the share of states with hazard warnings to roughly one-third. Larger states are better able to undertake such initiatives, because few firms can afford to ignore large-state markets. These warnings policies create an entry barrier to out-of-state firms and impede international trade.

• The wording of the California warning is inappropriate given the level of risk. Illinois consumers given this warning in a test situation viewed it as roughly comparable in severity to the cigarette warning, and they associated it with a lifetime cancer risk in excess of 0.1— that is, 10,000 times greater than the risk threshold under California's Proposition 65. The mismatch between the character of the warning and the actual risk level will impose substantial informational costs on consumers.

• Because a cancer warning or a reproductive-toxicity warning in one state may stigmatize the product in other states, industry officials believe that many firms will choose to reformulate products rather than to label them. The costs of reformulation cannot be predicted, since the role of the listed chemical within the product varies. But the associated costs of temporary product withdrawals may be immense. The 1969 cyclamate ban eliminated 50 percent of the total market for diet foods, and total diet-food sales were down by more than 40 percent even twenty weeks after the ban.

• Additional costs will be associated with testing products and printing labels. The extent of the labeling costs depends on the degree to which the packaging process is affected and the extent of the reformulation.

• Significant costs will be associated with labeling and distribution of products because of the need to segregate them in the distribution chain. For the five-state scenario, these costs are likely to be approximately 1–1.4 percent of total national product costs. In food costs alone, one out of fourteen products labeled in five states would impose annual labeling costs of $50 million. The bounty and penalty provisions under Proposition 65 also create the prospect of substantial additional costs if firms are not in compliance with the regulation.

2

State Warnings for Food, Drugs, Cosmetics, and Medical Devices

THE MAIN EVENT that has given rise to the debate over risk communication for food and drug products is California's Proposition 65, a statewide referendum. California voters who came to the polls on November 4, 1986, had to vote on an initiative entitled the "Safe Drinking Water and Toxic Enforcement Act of 1986."

California's Proposition 65

The requirements of this act were quite diverse. In addition to mandating hazard warnings for products that might pose a risk of carcinogenicity or reproductive toxicity, the act included warning requirements for environmental exposures and stipulations pertaining to pollution discharges in the state's waterways.

Significantly, the hazard-warnings aspects of the initiative, which are now the object of substantial policy debate, were not even regarded as a primary purpose of the act by those who voted for it. A California poll taken in October 1986, just before the voting, found that supporters of Proposition 65 gave as their reasons for support a variety of factors having little to do with hazard warnings. The breakdown of their reasons for supporting the measure is as follows:

- to protect our water/keep it clean—35 percent
- need to control, keep better track of toxic chemicals/know where chemicals are dumped—34 percent
- need to clean up toxic wastes/stop the polluters—16 percent
- toxics are getting out of control/too dangerous to people—13 percent

11

- need to safeguard our environment/will protect the environment—6 percent[1]

The reasons given in exit interviews on the day of the vote were quite similar. The breakdown of the reasons for support was as follows:

- to protect our water/keep it clean—72 percent
- to protect our environment—46 percent
- toxics are out of control/too dangerous—38 percent
- to keep better track of toxics/where they are—35 percent
- to stop the big polluters, the oil and chemical companies—1 percent[2]

None of these categories of response specifically mentions the role of hazard warnings. The desire to keep track of toxins, for example, pertains primarily to hazardous chemical wastes, such as those addressed by EPA's Superfund program, rather than to risk communication for consumer products. In short, the California voters were voting for a bundle of related environmental initiatives. Apparently a desire to institute a sweeping risk-communication program, requiring harsh warning statements for trace constituents of common consumer products, was not their intent. Nevertheless, the law remains in effect.

Under Proposition 65, California lists chemicals that state officials believe may be linked to possible risks of cancer or reproductive toxicity, typically using information from federal agencies and other external groups. For most listed substances, the state does not specify the acceptable level of exposure. A chemical's inclusion in the list does not signify that the particular exposure level to it in a given product is carcinogenic or has reproductive effects; only that *some* level of exposure may cause these effects in humans. The list may be based entirely on animal data.

For each chemical listed, the company must ascertain whether it is present in any of its products and, if so, it must decide whether the level of exposure poses a "significant" risk for cancer or is sufficiently below the "no-observable-effects" level for reproductive toxicants. If a company is unable to demonstrate either that a product contains no listed chemicals or that any listed chemical present is

---

[1]The Field Institute, the California poll, October 16, 1986, release no. 1366.

[2]The Field Institute, Opinion Index, vol. 6, December 1986.

below the applicable risk threshold, then it must provide warnings to consumers. The nature of these warnings requirements will be discussed further below.

Few warnings have appeared on consumer products to date. Warnings requirements have been imposed on alcoholic beverages through point-of-purchase displays. Tobacco products and selected other products bear on-product warnings. Generally, however, one notices little evidence of the effect of California's Proposition 65 upon entering a California grocery store or pharmacy.[3]

The reasons why apparently little activity has occurred are twofold. First, an interim standard currently exempts food, drugs, cosmetics, and medical devices that are in compliance with state and federal standards applicable to the product in question.[4] Under this rule, a product complying with the safety standards of the state and the FDA need not bear a warning label concerning listed carcinogens present in the product. The exemption was invalidated by a California trial court, however, in a suit brought by the AFL-CIO.[5] The reasoning behind the court's decision was that the intent of the act was to address all pertinent cancer and reproductive hazards, not simply those that are not regulated by federal agencies. Although the decision is on appeal, it is by no means certain that the exemption will remain. In the absence of the exemption, California's Proposition 65 will become much more consequential.

Second, although the exemption does not extend to reproductive toxicants, relatively few warnings have been required with respect to such chemicals because state actions to list them have occurred at a slower pace than that of actions to list carcinogens. Because the state criterion defining a reproductive toxicant is ten times more restrictive than the federal standard, as listing activities progress warning labels are likely to be required for a substantial number of products that

---

[3]There have also been signs posted in every grocery store upon entry, advising consumers to call a 1-800 number to receive information about products containing listed chemicals. Moreover, there was a large-scale advertising effort alerting consumers to the toll-free number system. But the initial effort to have the courts uphold the 1-800 system of risk communication was unsuccessful, and this case is currently on appeal before the Third District Court of Appeals, no. C007628 ICC v. Van De Kamp (Sacramento Superior Court no. 504601).

[4]Cal. Admin. Code Tit. 26, Sec. 22-12713.

[5]AFL-CIO v. Deukmejian, Sacramento Superior Court, no. 502541.

would satisfy federal safety standards.

The ultimate effect of California's Proposition 65 and similar initiatives is uncertain. Companies do not know what requirements they will have to meet and which products will be affected. The California science panel charged with the task of listing the chemicals will continue to modify this list, and companies must test their products to determine the presence of listed chemicals and ascertain that such levels are below the threshold for warning. Acquiring this knowledge for their current mixture of products would require extensive testing.

Much more difficult is trying to predict the effect of future requirements, since the chemicals that may be included in the future list are difficult to predict. This environment of uncertainty will have a chilling effect on product innovation. Firms will be reluctant to invest in new technologies or in products with ingredients that may be added to future chemical lists. The absence of a well-defined safe harbor imposes substantial costs on companies, which have already spent more than half a decade devoting resources to compliance with this and related initiatives.

If California's Proposition 65 required warnings only when products failed to satisfy federal safety standards, firms could have greater certainty regarding their compliance status. But the stipulations of Proposition 65 and other initiatives generally differ from the federally imposed safety requirements, and they may impose warnings on products that satisfy federal safety standards.

Under Proposition 65, once a company has determined that a listed chemical is present in its product, the company must either conduct an analysis to establish that the exposure through the product is below the risk threshold and requires no warning, or reformulate a product that contains a listed chemical. If adequate data are unavailable to establish that the exposure requires no warning, or if reformulation is not feasible, manufacturers must provide a warning.

The company would have a substantial incentive to comply with the law, since the law imposes substantial penalties on a manufacturer for each exposure for which it was responsible and failed to provide a required warning. The law may be enforced by private citizens as well as by the state. Because warnings are presumptively required for any amount of a listed chemical, it is the burden of the manufacturer to conduct the research and analyses necessary to show

14

that the particular exposure occurring through its product does not exceed the risk threshold and is exempt from the warning requirement.

This burden of research and analysis will be most modest in the case of drugs and medical devices that are currently the subject of FDA pre-market approval requirements. These regulations entail extensive characterization of the chemical constituents of the product and scientific data supporting their safety.

In contrast, the company's burden to develop data and analyze them will be heavier for such chemicals as over-the-counter drugs and food additives. For these chemicals, a company would be required to obtain from the FDA the safety data upon which the FDA's approval was based and to verify them. Once the FDA has sanctioned these substances and defined safe conditions of use, manufacturers of finished products may use the chemicals in accordance with approved conditions without developing independent safety data and pre-market approval. The greatest burden will be for foods and their natural constituents. Manufacturers are not required, under federal standards, to identify and characterize all chemical constituents of food before marketing.

In situations where the FDA requirements have been met, these standards would be more stringent than the California regulations. The FDA's predominant risk standard for carcinogens is a lifetime risk of 1/1,000,000, which is ten times as conservative as the 1/100,000 lifetime risk embodied in California's Proposition 65. In contrast, the Proposition 65 risk threshold for reproductive toxicants is ten times as conservative as the FDA standard. In the case of reproductive toxicity, compliance with FDA pre-market approval requirements would not ensure compliance with the California requirements. Based on these patterns, the greatest burdens would fall on the companies in the areas of food products and over-the-counter drugs not subject to the pre-market approval requirements, for risks associated with reproductive toxicity.

Two features of the implemented regulations for Proposition 65 are noteworthy. First, on-product labels are not required for alcoholic beverages, as an in-store sign for the entire alcoholic beverage section will suffice. The California wine industry consequently will not be stigmatized by warning labels, even though wine contains both carcinogens and reproductive toxicants. Second, in recognition of

15

pressures from the powerful agricultural interests, naturally occurring carcinogens are also exempt. Aflatoxin mold on peanuts that arises in the course of normal peanut production will consequently be excluded from concern, even though the risk posed by natural carcinogens may far exceed the trace carcinogens covered by Proposition 65.

Summary of State Warnings Regulations

Table 2–1 summarizes the various initiatives throughout the country related to Proposition 65 and similar warnings efforts. The first column of warnings regulations listed includes Proposition 65 types of measures. In addition to the original Proposition 65 enacted in California in 1986, eight states have considered or are currently considering a Proposition 65 type of proposal. In each case the most recent proposal is listed, where these proposals have reached the stage of bills formally proposed or draft legislation being discussed in state legislatures.

Perhaps the most noteworthy feature of this list of states is that it includes several—California, Illinois, New York, and Ohio—with large and influential consumer populations. If these states alone were to adopt a Proposition 65 type of measure, that would influence a substantial portion of the national market for these products.

The size of the states that adopt Proposition 65 types of measures also affects the dynamics of the policy development. A major concern for companies is whether there will be a flurry of states that follow California's lead. One would expect, for example, that policy action by New York will be more influential than such action by South Dakota. Actions by states with large national markets will make it easier for smaller states to adopt similar measures, with less fear that companies will simply choose to exit the market in these states.

This relationship between state size and the undertaking of Proposition 65 types of initiatives is not perfect, but it also reflects economic factors likely to influence such measures. Indeed, the pivotal role of large states is likely to be a recurring phenomenon in the federalism debate. If states such as Alaska or Rhode Island, for example, were to take the lead with a Proposition 65 type of measure that imposed substantial burdens on firms, then national firms could easily choose simply not to market their products in these states.

TABLE 2–1
STATUS OF STATE WARNINGS REGULATIONS, 1991

State	Proposition 65 Type of Measure	BST (Bovine Somatotropin)	Other Product Warnings
California	Enacted, 1986		Environmental, raw oysters, raw milk
Hawaii	Proposed, 1989		
Illinois	Proposed, 1991		
Maine		Proposal, 1991, to prohibit sale	
Massachusetts	In study, 1990		
Minnesota		Warnings proposal, 1991	
Missouri	Proposed, 1988		
New York	Proposed, 1991	Warnings proposal, 1991	Over-the-counter drugs label for risk to over age 60
Ohio	Proposed, 1991		
Oregon	Proposed, 1988		
Pennsylvania			Ibuprofen label for adverse side effects
South Dakota		Warnings proposal, 1991	
Tennessee	Proposed, 1988		
Wisconsin		Statute, 1990, temporary ban on use, 1991 proposal to extend ban	

NOTE: This list was current as of August 1991.
SOURCE: Author.

Doing so would cost them little. If, however, a major state such as California or New York were to take action, then ignoring the ramifications of the measure would not be discretionary. Selling to this market may affect the viability of the product line and the firm.

The second column of warnings regulations listed pertains to bovine somatotropin (BST). The risk-policy concern is over the level of BST in dairy products, not the presence of it. BST is a naturally occurring growth hormone in cows and is often present in milk, dairy products, meat, and meat byproducts. It is the use of supplemental BST in cows to enhance milk production that is under investigation. The FDA has authorized the consumption of products derived from cows who have received supplemental BST. Three states, however—Minnesota, New York, and South Dakota—have proposed that warnings be required on these products. Wisconsin has enacted a statute that at least temporarily bans the use of BST, and Maine has proposed a similar measure. The Maine and Wisconsin actions are more extensive than risk-communication efforts. The option of withdrawing products, however, is a likely response to the hazard-warning requirements under Proposition 65 types of measures, and as a consequence it will be included among the full set of warnings regulations proposed.

The BST initiatives by dairy states such as Wisconsin and Minnesota are consistent with interest-group models of regulatory activity. Dairy states have an economic incentive to control the use of chemicals that will limit production, particularly for products such as agricultural goods that are often in surplus and carry prices that have been sufficiently low to warrant price support. A second version of the interest-group explanation is that the presence of BST, which remains an object of scientific and public controversy, may generate the same kind of public alarm as did Alar in apples. Dairy farmers consequently may be willing to sacrifice some short-run profits to avoid the risk of dramatic losses if BST were to become a major target of concern.

The final column in table 2–1 summarizes the other kinds of warnings programs that have been enacted. Under Proposition 65 the state of California imposed general environmental-warning requirements for carcinogenic exposures. Gas stations, for example, must post signs at the pump advising consumers of the risks posed by gasoline fumes. In addition, California has adopted a regulation requiring retail-food facilities that sell raw oysters from the Gulf of Mexico to post a warning informing individuals that eating raw oysters can cause illness or death in individuals who have liver disease, cancer, or a weakness of the immune system. Similarly, California has a warning for unpasteurized milk and dairy products, highlighting the risk from disease-causing microorganisms.

New York has proposed a warnings requirement for over-the-counter drugs, urging that users more than sixty years of age consult their physician or pharmacist prior to use of the product. Finally, Pennsylvania has a warnings proposal for ibuprofen, which would mandate a label or a package insert alerting users to its adverse effects.

Table 2–1 makes it clear that state warnings efforts have begun to proliferate. Moreover, there are substantial differences among the states in the warnings requirements being imposed. Some states have opted for a Proposition 65 type of measure, others have favored a BST warning, and others have opted for a grab bag of product-specific warnings. Moreover, even where individual states have supported a Proposition 65 measure, the specific measures being supported may differ.

The result is that firms will face an increasingly different combination of state regulatory requirements, which will impose substantial costs on those that operate beyond a local basis. The nature of these requirements and the potential disruption they will generate is the focus of the subsequent chapters.

3

Policy Scope and Warnings Criteria

THIS CHAPTER examines the extent of coverage of Proposition 65 types of measures.

Product Coverage of State Labeling Regulations

The BST and other product-warning regulations indicated in table 2–1 have quite specific coverage. They apply to dairy products, raw oysters, and various over-the-counter drugs.

The scope of Proposition 65 types of measures is also quite diverse. Although many of these proposed bills are patterned after California's Proposition 65, the products included vary depending on the state.

Table 3–1 summarizes the product coverage of the various Proposition 65 types of measures. On paper the California bill is comprehensive, applying to food, drugs, cosmetics, medical devices, and other consumer products. In practice, the extent of the coverage will depend on whether the exemption for products regulated by the FDA, which has recently been overturned by the courts, will ultimately be upheld. If this exemption is upheld, many of the components of the first four categories listed in table 3–1 will be exempt from coverage. At present, the main effect of this regulation is to influence the "other" consumer products category: alcoholic beverages, tobacco products, and household chemical products.

The coverage in New York and Ohio is similar, except that services are also included in Ohio. In these states there is no explicit exemption for products in conformance with FDA regulations. Such an exemption was not included in the original Proposition 65 initiative, but it was added as part of the implementing regulations issued

20

TABLE 3–1
PRODUCT COVERAGE OF STATE LABELING REGULATIONS

State	Food	Drugs	Cosmetics	Medical Devices	Other Consumer Products
California	Yes	Yes	Yes	Yes	Yes
New York	Yes	Yes	Yes	Yes	Yes
Ohio	Yes	Yes	Yes	Yes	Yes, and includes services
Massachusetts	Yes	Yes	Yes	Yes	Yes
Illinois	Yes	No	No	No	Yes, only food packaging

SOURCE: Author.

by California. Unless there is a comparable effort to limit the scope of the New York and Ohio initiatives, their coverage may in fact be greater than that of California.[1]

In all likelihood, the Massachusetts Proposition 65 type of measure will also have broad coverage, although the exact status of drugs, cosmetics, and medical devices has yet to be determined.

The final Proposition 65 type of measure listed in table 3–1 is that of Illinois. That measure would be restricted to food and food packaging. Drugs, cosmetics, and medical devices would not be included under the scope of that effort.

The coverage of all these regulations remains tentative. Excepting that for California, all the information in table 3–1 is based on legislative proposals. These legislative proposals change over time. In Illinois, for example, three different bills were introduced in 1991 and none has yet been approved.

Thresholds for Warnings

For each of the products listed in table 3–1, the company must either reformulate the product to eliminate the hazardous ingredients or provide a suitable warning. The risk criteria that influence whether a

---

[1]The Ohio bill is a voter initiative, as was California's. Supporters are attempting to get the Ohio measure on the November 1992 ballot.

TABLE 3–2
RISK THRESHOLDS FOR WARNINGS, 1991

State	For Cancer	For Reproductive Toxicity	Chemicals Warned Against
California	"No significant risk," excess lifetime cancer risk of 1/100,000[a]	No observable effect at 1,000 × level in question	Chemicals in labor code, EPA, International Agency for Research on Cancer (IARC), National Toxicology Program (NTP), Federal government carcinogens or reproductive toxicants, and state's "qualified experts" listing
New York	Unspecified	Unspecified	State's "qualified experts" listing, state or federal listing, or other authoritative bodies
Ohio	"No significant risk," excess lifetime cancer risk of 1/1,000,000[b]	No observable effect at 1,000 × risk level if reproductive toxicity; otherwise, at 100 × level	Director of Environmental Protection listing or listing by one of five agencies—NTP, EPA, NIOSH, FDA, or IARC

Massachusetts	"No significant risk" from lifetime exposure	"Ample margin of safety"; no observable effect at 1,000 × level, but no observable effect at 100 × level if data complete and reliable	Department of Health listing, federal government, and other authoritative bodies
Illinois	"No significant risk" from lifetime exposure	"No significant risk" from lifetime exposure; no observable effect at 1,000 × level under H.B. 208	Chemicals identified by state's qualified experts, NTP, IARC, and other "authoritative bodies"

a. One case of cancer per 100,000 product users over lifetime product use.
b. One diagnosed case per 1 million users.
SOURCE: Author.

warning must be provided are delineated in table 3–2, which provides the threshold for cancer-risk communication, the threshold for risk communication pertaining to reproductive toxicity, and the provisions pertaining to state lists of chemicals covered by the regulation.

Consider first the cancer-risk threshold. Proposition 65 types of measures specify that the product must pose "no significant risk" in every instance, with the exception of New York, for which there is no specified risk threshold. In the case of California, the "no-significant-risk" criterion has been linked to a risk threshold of 1/100,000, whereas for Ohio the risk threshold is a 1/1,000,000 lifetime cancer risk. The difference between 1/100,000 and 1/1,000,000 is a factor of 10—a large discrepancy with respect to the level of risk. The relationship between "no significant risk" and the particular risk level is a matter of state discretion.

Nevertheless, we do have some precedent in that regard. The dominant risk threshold for FDA decision making pertaining to carcinogens is 1/1,000,000.[2] But the FDA does not routinely focus on risk levels alone. The emphasis of FDA policies is on risk-benefit analysis for drugs, whereas Proposition 65 focuses only on risk without recognizing that trade-offs matter. Consumers can, of course, make these trade-offs after being provided the information, but the warnings approach is mismatched to the levels of risk involved.

The lifetime risk threshold of 1/100,000 adopted by California is calculated based on a lifetime exposure to a product, where the state specifies a normal life span of seventy years. To put this risk in perspective, it implies that the annual risk must be at least 1/7,000,000 for the product to be above the risk threshold. If an individual would normally consume this product on a daily basis, then the risk at each time of use is even less—1/2,555,000,000, or less than one chance in 2 billion of acquiring cancer from any given episode of product consumption.

Determining whether chemicals in their products are below the risk threshold will be the responsibility of the companies. Thus, the state will not typically specify an accepted dose-response rate. Extrapolation from animal studies to humans is an exercise fraught with error. Moreover, as practiced in the federal government, these

---

[2]See, for example, 38 Fed. Reg. 19226 (July 19, 1973).

procedures are also biased upward. The emphasis is on the most sensitive animal species, for example, rather than on the species that would be the most reliable predictor of the risk in humans.

The effect of these risk levels on knowledgeable consumers should be small. A useful index of the importance of providing warnings of the risks addressed by Proposition 65 is to ask, to what degree would knowledge of these risks alter purchase decisions? Suppose that in making their own decisions individuals placed a value on risks to their lives of $4 million per expected life, which is consistent with the labor-market evidence on the implicit value of life.[3] If these individuals purchased a product posing a lifetime risk of 1/100,000 and if this product were consumed weekly, then knowledge of the risk should influence their weekly willingness to pay for the product by less than one penny. Similarly, a product consumed daily with a lifetime risk of 1/100,000 would command a willingness to pay for a safer product of under 1/7¢. In effect, if this small risk were processed in a reliable fashion, it should have a negligible effect on consumer behavior. Risks with such a low potential impact on consumer willingness to pay might better be classified as *de minimis*, rather than as at the threshold of significance.

The conditions for requiring warnings on substances that have reproductive effects are even more stringent. There the test is not whether a significant risk of harm is present. Rather than being concerned with adverse effects, all the reproductive-toxicity standards focus on "observable effects." Thus, any effect—even those not shown to be adverse—would justify a label of "reproductive toxicant" under these regulations. Vitamin A is one such chemical ingredient that has reproductive effects at sufficiently high doses.

Achieving zero observable effects is not, however, sufficient cause to meet the requirements of these measures. The dominant criterion, which has been adopted by California and proposed in Ohio, Massachusetts, and Illinois, is to require that there be no observable effects at 1,000 times the exposure level in question. This is a thousandfold factor of conservatism below the no-effects level.

---

[3]See W. Kip Viscusi, *Fatal Tradeoffs: Public and Private Responsibilities for Risk* (New York: Oxford University Press, 1992). In addition, assume a length of life of seventy years and a real rate of interest (that is, nominal rate of interest minus the inflation rate) between 0 and 2 percent.

25

For all risk reductions below no risk whatsoever, society will perhaps pay substantial costs with no associated benefits. Viewed differently, this policy implies that we are willing to place an infinite value on the associated health effects.

Moreover, this conservatism factor augments other risk assessment biases in the same direction. Current risk-analysis procedures used by government agencies mix risk management with science. The usual procedures place the greatest weight on the upper end of the 95 percent confidence limit of the risk range, rather than on the mean value of the risk. Additional conservatism-adjustment factors are added when the evidence is uncertain. The California Scientific Advisory Panel, which advises the governor on Proposition 65, concluded that the thousandfold safety factor for reproductive toxicants was "scientifically indefensible" applied across the board to all chemicals and all products.[4] Nevertheless, the reliance on these arbitrary risk-scale factors continues.

There is some modification of this reproductive-toxicity requirement in several states. Ohio adopts the thousandfold safety factor for reproductive effects, but only a factor of one hundred if the substance in the products is not known to cause reproductive toxicity. Massachusetts utilizes a safety factor of one hundred if the available data are complete and reliable. Thus, even with the best available data indicating that the product poses no risk of reproductive toxicity, meeting that level is not sufficient. The firm must show that one hundred times this level of exposure also would pose no risk of any reproductive effects, either positive or negative. Finally, Illinois adopts the thousandfold safety factor under one of the pieces of legislation that have been proposed.

Under these different initiatives, it is the responsibility of the company to determine which products meet the risk threshold and which do not. The states have established procedures for listing potentially risky chemicals. The company must then determine whether a given chemical present in its product violates the risk threshold either for cancer or for reproductive toxicity. The states specify the critical-risk probability and the chemicals to be considered, but the firms have the often enormous task of assessing

---

[4]Letter from Scientific Advisory Panel chairman, Wendell Kilgore, to Assemblyman Bill Jones, January 5, 1989.

exposure levels and pertinent dose-response relationships. Burdens normally shared by federal regulators become the sole responsibility of industry.

The procedures for inclusion of a chemical on the list of candidates for warnings are outlined in the final column of table 3–2. In every case some state body, such as a scientific advisory board or the state's department of environmental health, will spearhead the listing process. This group will not only utilize its own judgment but will also draw upon the activities of other agencies. The chief ones cited are the EPA, the International Agency for Research on Cancer (IARC), the National Toxicology Program (NTP), the National Institute of Occupational Safety and Health (NIOSH), and the FDA. As a practical matter, most states have little scientific expertise in these matters and will be forced to rely upon the results of other agencies to determine which products should be listed.

Listed Chemicals in California

In every case, the states have indicated that they will provide a list of chemicals to the firms, after which the firms must assess exposure levels and show that warnings are not needed. A partial list of potential carcinogens designated thus far by California appears in Table 3–3, and selected reproductive and developmental toxicants appear in table 3–4. These tables also describe the nature of the likely risk exposure. The appendix presents the complete California chemical list as of July 1991. The process of listing chemicals is continuous, so firms face a steadily increasing menu of substances on the list. This list is especially likely to increase as scientific techniques for identifying the presence of low-probability risks become more sophisticated. The standard for reproductive toxicity is linked to "no observable effects." What is observable will pertain to an increasingly low risk level, as our risk-measurement technology becomes more refined. In earlier years, we were less able to distinguish chemicals that posed low-probability risks because our scientific basis for making such assessments was less refined. In the future we may be able to measure effects that are so minor they should be ignored.

Many of the chemicals appearing in table 3–3 that are likely to affect the categories of food and other products covered by Proposi-

TABLE 3–3
Exposure to Selected California Proposition 65 Carcinogens

Listed Chemical	Source of Exposure
A-alpha-C	Can be formed in processed protein food
Acetaldehyde	Naturally occurring, used in manufacture of chemicals, perfumes, dyes, flavors, plastics, etc.
Acrylonitrile	Plastics
Aflatoxins	Naturally occurring mycotoxin produced by fungi in food, such as peanuts
Alachlor	Herbicide for grasses
Aldrin	Formerly used insecticide, in soil
Arsenic	Herbicide for nonfood use, contaminated shellfish and plants grown in sludge
Asbestos	Insulation, talc, plastics
Benzene	Solvent
Benzo[b]fluoranthene	Smoke, smoked foods, and liquid smoke
Benzo[j]fluoranthene	Smoke, smoked foods, and liquid smoke
Benzo[k]fluoranthene	Smoke, smoked foods, and liquid smoke
Benzo[a]fluoranthene	Smoke, smoked foods, and liquid smoke
Butylated hydroxyanisole	Antioxidant approved for food use
Cadmium and cadmium components	Environmental contaminant
Captafol	Fungicide for apples, vegetables, potatoes, field crops, and seed treatment
Captan	Fungicide for apples, deciduous fruit, home use, lacquers, paper, and cosmetic preservative
Carbon tetrachloride	Environmental contaminant; was used in fumigants for grain, nuts, and dry food products; solvent for adhesives
Chlordane	Insecticide for underground termite control
Chlordecone	Formerly used insecticide; contaminant in fish and seafood
Chlordimeform	Insecticide, formerly found in cotton seed oil, meat, poultry, eggs, and dairy products

28

TABLE 3–3 (continued)

Listed Chemical	Source of Exposure
Chloroform	Environmental contaminant, can result from chlorinated water
Chrysene	See dibenz[a,h] acridine
Cinnamyl anthranilate	Widely used flavor and fragrance in food, beverages, soap, detergents, and perfumes
Daminozide	Herbicide and plant growth regulator; food use of Alar, 85% water soluble powder, canceled; formerly used on apples, peaches, cherries, nectarines, tomatoes, and Brussels sprouts
DDD	Environmental contaminant
DDE	Environmental contaminant
DDT	Environmental contaminant; banned insecticide, but residues exist
DDVP	Insecticide for household pests; in plastic strips, no-pest strips, and flea collars
Dibenz[a,h]acridine	Environmental contaminant formed in hydrocarbon process such as coke oven burning
Dibenz[a,j]acridine	See dibenz[a,h]acridine
Dibenz[a,h]anthracene	See dibenz[a,h]acridine
7-HDibenzo[c,g]carbazole	See dibenz[a,h]acridine
Dibenzo[a,e]pyrene	See dibenz[a,h]acridine; detected in foods from mineral oil and waxes used as release agents in food containers; FDA studies show no health hazard
Dibenzo[a,i]pyrene	See dibenz[a,h]acridine
1,2-Dibromo-3-chloropropane	Soil fumigant, exposure through drinking water
p-Dichlorobenzene	Insecticidal fumigant in toilet bowl deodorants, moth flakes, contaminated drinking water, and fish

(Table continues)

29

TABLE 3–3 (continued)

Listed Chemical	Source of Exposure
Dieldrin	Discontinued pesticide; residues in food, water, and fish
7,12-Dimethylbenz(a) anthracene	See dibenz[a,h]acridine
1,4-Dioxane	Solvent for dyes, lacquers, varnishes, waxes, and mineral oil
Ethyl-4,4'dichlorobenzilate	Insecticide found in fruit and vegetable peels
Ethylene dibromide	Fumigant banned in U.S. but on some imported soil samples
Ethylene oxide	Spices and nuts fumigant
Ethylene thiourea	Accelerator for curing of elastomers
Folpet	Fungicide on fruits, vegetables, flowers, paints, plastics, and building interiors
Formaldehyde (gas)	Resins; emissions from stoves, insulation, and resin-coated rugs; naturally occurring in foods, also a contaminant
Glu-P-1	Protein pyrolysate, can be formed in processed protein food
Glu-P-2	Protein pyrolysate, can be formed in processed protein food
Glycidaldehyde	Finishing of wool and oil tanning; occurs in sunflower oil and rancid lard
Heptachlor	Insecticide, registration canceled but residues remain
Heptachlor epoxide	Metabolically formed from heptachlor; found in dairy products, meat, fish, and poultry
Hexachlorobenzene	Raw material in synthetic rubber; contaminated food and drinking water
Hexachlorocyclohexane	See lindane; imported foods, etc.
Hexachlorodibenzodioxin	Impurity in 2,4,5-T (Agent Orange); fly ash from municipal waste
Ideno[1,2,3-cd]pyrene	Research chemical; combustion of coal, wood, cigarettes; found in rain, drinking water, and diverse foods

TABLE 3–3 (continued)

Listed Chemical	Source of Exposure
Lactofen	Herbicide Cobra, to control broadleaf weeds
Lindane	Insecticide for field crops (corn, wheat), pasture, livestock, etc.
Mancozeb	Fungicide for vegetables, field crops, deciduous fruits, and nuts
Maneb	Fungicide; see mancozeb
Me-A-alpha-C	Protein pyrolysate, can be formed in processed protein food
5-Methylchrysene	Similar to dibenz[a,h]acridine
Methyl iodide	Used in pharmaceutical intermediate preparation. Marine seafood
Metiram	See mancozeb
N-Nitroso-n-butylamine	Nitrate treated products: baby pacifiers, rubber nipples, cigarette smoke, air inside new cars
N-Nitrosodiethanolamine	See N-Nitroso-n-butylamine
N-Nitrosodiethylamine	See N-Nitroso-n-butylamine
N-Nitrosodimethylamine	See N-Nitroso-n-butylamine
p-Nitrosodiphenylamine	See N-Nitroso-n-butylamine
N-Nitrosodiphenylamine	See N-Nitroso-n-butylamine
N-Nitrosodi-n-propylamine	See N-Nitroso-n-butylamine
N-Nitroso-N-ethylurea	See N-Nitroso-n-butylamine
N-Nitrosomethylethylamine	See N-Nitroso-n-butylamine
N-Nitroso-N-methylurea	See N-Nitroso-n-butylamine
N-Nitroso-N-methylurethane	See N-Nitroso-n-butylamine
N-Nitrosomethylvinylamine	See N-Nitroso-n-butylamine
N-Nitrosomorpholine	See N-Nitroso-n-butylamine
N-Nitrosonornicotine	See N-Nitroso-n-butylamine
N-Nitrosopiperidine	See N-Nitroso-n-butylamine
N-Nitrosopyrrolidine	See N-Nitroso-n-butylamine
N-Nitrososarcosine	See N-Nitroso-n-butylamine
Norethisterone	Medication: oral contraceptives, progestin

(Table continues)

31

TABLE 3–3 (continued)

Listed Chemical	Source of Exposure
Polychlorinated biphenyls	Electric cable and wire insulation; environmental contaminant in paper used for food packaging
Polychlorinated biphenyls (PCB 60% or more chlorine)	No U.S. production after 1977; food, drinking water, and fish
Potassium bromate	Dough improver in flour and baking products
Propylene oxide	Various uses, such as in modified food starch; found in heated foods, automobile exhaust
Sterigamatocystin	Fungal toxin
2,3,7,8-Tetrachlorodibenzo-paradioxin	Herbicide contaminant
2,4,6 Trichlorophenol	Formerly an herbicide; municipal waste particulate and in drinking water
Trichloroethylene	Solvent is exempt; color additives for food, drugs, and cosmetics; traces in meat, beverages, dairy products, produce, and oils
Trp-P-1	Protein pyrolysate, formed in processed protein food
Trp-P-2	Protein pyrolysate, formed in processed protein food
Urethane	Occurs when diethylpyrocarbonate (preservative used in wine, fruit juices, and soft drinks) is added to aqueous solutions; occurs in fermented foods
Zineb	See mancozeb

SOURCE: Adapted and rewritten by the author based on the National Food Processors Association, "Possible Sources of Human Exposure to Proposition 65 Listed Chemicals," April 5, 1990.

TABLE 3–4
EXPOSURES TO DEVELOPMENTAL TOXICANTS AND REPRODUCTIVE
TOXICANTS, SELECTED CALIFORNIA PROPOSITION 65 CHEMICALS

Toxicant	Source of Exposure
Developmental Toxicant	
Chlordecone	Lawn and shrub insecticide
Dinoseb	Herbicide, pesticide banned in the U.S.
Ethylene glycol monoethyl ether	Adhesives
Ethylene glycol monomethyl ether	Adhesives
Hexachlorobenzene	Raw material for synthetic rubber, plasticizer; ambient air, drinking water, food
Methyl mercury	Environmental contaminant, especially seafood
Female reproductive toxicant	
Ethylene oxide	Fumigant for spices, tobacco, furs, bedding, hospital sterilization, and cosmetic sterilization
Lead	Environmental contaminant; in old cars and paints
1-2-Dibromo-3-Chloropropane	Extensively used as soil fumigant in California; residues in soil and water
Dinoseb	Herbicide, insecticide banned in the U.S.
Ethylene glycol monoethyl ether	Adhesives
Ethylene glycol monomethyl ether	Adhesives

SOURCE: Adapted and rewritten by the author based on the National Food Processors Association, "Possible Sources of Human Exposure to Proposition 65 Listed Chemicals," April 5, 1990.

tion 65 are pesticides. Some of these pesticides are used directly on the products; others may have been used and may now be present in the soil. Fumigants and other chemicals, such as those used as dyes, also appear on the list.

The list in table 3–4 of reproductive toxicants is less developed. The brevity of this list indicates not that fewer chemicals will be covered by this standard but that the review of potential reproductive toxicants is in an early stage.

The traditional focus of government agencies such as the EPA and the Occupational Safety and Health Administration (OSHA) has been on carcinogens rather than on reproductive toxicants. These policies in turn have influenced the nature of scientific research. As future research methods become better able to identify reproductive toxicants and as the scope of research becomes expanded over time, this list should become even longer than that of carcinogens, because of the stringent margins of safety of its risk criteria and because of the linkage of the test to observable effects rather than potential adverse effects.

The problem facing a company that produces food products is daunting. These lists include a large number of pesticides and herbicides. Some of these are applied directly on crops; others are present in the soil. If all food companies grew their own crops, they would have greater control over the presence of these chemicals. But food products are generally purchased from a variety of suppliers, both domestic and international.

Many firms are already knowledgeable about pesticide use. Even with contract growers, the particular pesticide and its time of application are usually known to the producer. But imports may be less certain. Proposition 65 and related measures shift a substantial burden on the food producer to ascertain that its products meet all the exposure requirements.

The regulatory program has been set up so that any producer of food, drugs, medical devices, or cosmetics can be challenged in court with respect to the presence of one or more of the chemicals listed. It will be the task of the company to prove that its product is safe. The prospect of nuisance suits and the costs they impose is substantial.

Companies cannot treat any such suits lightly, because the penalty provisions are considerable. The cap on penalties is $2,500 per day, per violation, in California. Daily state consumption of the product by 100,000 consumers could imply a limit of $250,000,000 per day, if each consumption decision is treated as a separate violation under the bounty-hunter provision. How the courts will ultimately link these penalty provisions to the extent of the product's use has not yet been resolved.

Acceptable Warnings Methods

Companies that sell products containing listed chemicals and that wish to avoid these lawsuits have three alternatives. First, they can ensure that their products meet the criteria delineated under Proposition 65. Doing so may be difficult, particularly with respect to pesticide residues and trace carcinogens.

Second, a company that cannot ensure that its product meets the Proposition 65 criteria can reformulate the product to come under the guidelines. This could take the form of product testing to guarantee that the pesticide residues are below the allowable limit. A more extreme variant on the reformulation option is to withdraw the product from the market. The producer can choose to sell the product in the remaining states and simply to abandon the California market. As will be shown below, this option has the drawback of foreclosing a major national market. The third option is to adopt the mode of warnings stipulated for products that do not meet the criteria for exemption from warning under Proposition 65 and related measures.

Table 3–5 indicates the acceptable modes of warning and content of warning that may be adopted in the different states. In general, the states give the firm a variety of mechanisms from which they may select: on-product labels, posting of notices at the store, shelf labels, advertising, and toll-free services. These are possible options, but there is no guarantee that use of any single mechanism will satisfy the firm's obligation to provide adequate warning. In some instances specific options are ruled out, such as the telephone in Massachusetts. Other states, such as Illinois, are quite specific about how the shelf labels should appear if they are used. In California, where there are diverse options, reliance on them has not proved sufficient. The food industry, for example, originally adopted an approach that combined an in-store notification of a 1-800

TABLE 3–5
ACCEPTABLE WARNINGS METHODS

State	Mode of Warning	Content of Warning
California	May include product labels, posting of notices, notices in media, shelf labels, signs, advertising, and toll-free services	Safe harbor warning: "WARNING: this product contains a chemical known to the state of California to cause cancer." "WARNING: This product contains a chemical known to the state of California to cause birth defects or other reproductive harm."
New York	Product labels, posted notices, or notices in the news media	Unspecified
Ohio	Prominent display on a label or, if infeasible, shelf labeling, signs, or other communication at retail outlet	State-specific required warning: "WARNING: This product contains one or more toxic substances known to cause cancer." "WARNING: This product contains toxic chemicals known to cause birth defects or other reproductive harm."
Massachusetts	On-product labels and display affixed to a product; specifically excludes telephones	Unspecified

TABLE 3–5 (continued)

State	Mode of Warning	Content of Warning
Illinois	Product labels, shelf labels near posted price, menu, or list of products	State-specific required warning: "WARNING: this product contains a chemical known to the state of Illinois to cause cancer." "WARNING: This product contains a chemical known to the state of Illinois to cause birth defects or other reproductive harm."

SOURCE: Author.

number, a toll-free system for obtaining information regarding products posing designated risks under Proposition 65, and extensive advertising of the toll-free number system. The industry's initial attempt to have the courts rule that this approach complies with Proposition 65 was unsuccessful.

The various options that involve in-store displays and shelf labels have thus far proved infeasible. Adding shelf labels would clutter the appearance of the grocery stores, which would impose marketing costs on the store beyond the labor and nuisance costs of installing and maintaining the labels. In addition, the cost would be borne by the grocery stores rather than the producers, creating a practical problem that would diminish the acceptability of this option. Since the ultimate responsibility for warning rests with the producer, grocery store operators have been understandably reluctant to incur these costs unilaterally or to share this responsibility.

One might well wonder why the producers do not simply contract with grocery store operators to post in-store displays. This was done on a limited basis for the toll-free-number warning approach that the courts found to be in compliance. One barrier to this option is the potentially high transactions cost of negotiating agreements with a large number of decentralized stores, which may be affected differently by extensive in-store warnings. A second difficulty is the hold-up problem. A small segment of stores may demand substantial compensation, knowing that the producer needs their compliance. There are limits to such a strategy, however, since the producer can simply refrain from selling its products at those stores.

More important, the ultimate legal burdens will be borne by the producing firms. If a grocery store operator fails to post a shelf label, perhaps because it has been inadvertently knocked down by a customer, then the responsibility for providing an adequate warning would continue to rest with the manufacturers. Most laws hold the retailer liable, but they give priority to enforcement against manufacturers.

Largely because of these costs, the industry has sought to achieve approval for the toll-free information system. Another approach, which has been adopted for alcoholic beverages, is a sign indicating that all products of that class pose potential risks. Such a sweeping warning is appropriate for alcoholic beverages, because there is no differentiation in the risk among products. But one could not post a similar sign in the produce section, since all produce items do not pose the same risk. Ultimately, compliance with the regulation will require some product-specific warning mechanism that is the responsibility of the producing firm. Unless the courts reverse themselves and approve the toll-free service approach, or unless the state regulators indicate that other approaches are acceptable, such as the placement in stores of lists of the products that violate Proposition 65, probably the mode of compliance of choice will focus on the product-labeling option.

Suppose a firm has decided to place a warning on the product. The specific warning it can select is often dictated under these measures. The accepted wording under Proposition 65 appears in the final column of table 3–5. This warning can be viewed as a safe-harbor warning, in that the firm can be confident that it has complied with Proposition 65 if it adopts this wording. A firm can adopt some other wording, but it runs the risk of being found in noncompliance. Telling consumers that the lifetime risk is only 1/100,000, for example, may be viewed as an attempt to undercut the warning even though the statement is true.

The character of the current warning in California is quite stringent: "WARNING: This product contains a chemical known to the state of California to cause cancer." As we will see below, this warning is comparable in severity to the cigarette warning after which it has apparently been patterned. It is noteworthy that this wording had never been tested on consumers to ascertain that it did imply risks of the magnitude specified under Proposition 65. One of the costs of the regulation, documented below, is the imposition of substantial informational costs on consumers, who will form incorrect perceptions of the risk posed by the product.

This problem is perhaps even more severe with respect to the warnings in the states of Ohio and Illinois. These states permit no discretion on the part of the firm, which must adopt the specific warning mandated under the proposal. The Illinois warning is identical to the California one, except for the state name. The Ohio warning is somewhat different in that it makes reference to "one or more toxic substances known to cause cancer" rather than to "a chemical known . . . to cause cancer."

Firms considering compliance with these regulations consequently cannot use the same warning in every state. The Illinois warning is specific and would not be acceptable in any other state. The California safe-harbor wording would suffice in California and elsewhere, but changing the state name would require a separate printing. There is no indication that in either case the firm can omit the phrases pertaining to the particular state so as to use a common warning in different states.

Even if that were acceptable, the wording in Illinois and California differs from that in Ohio, since it pertains not simply to one chemical but possibly to multiple toxic substances. Firms consequently cannot adopt a common wording and achieve compliance in all these jurisdictions.

To ensure compliance, the firm would have to adopt a separate warning program for each state, which would entail a separate labeling effort for products being shipped to each state.

National Market Share Affected

Many of the states represented in the list of those adopting or considering hazard warnings programs are among the largest ones. For this reason, firms are less able to avoid the warnings effort by withdrawing a product from the state and losing the market. Consequently there is a greater chance that the warnings effort will induce

TABLE 3–6
NATIONAL MARKET SHARE OF STATES WITH LABELING REGULATIONS
AND PROPOSALS
(percent)

State	Drugs	Grocery Products
California	14.65	12.15
Hawaii	n.a.	n.a.
Illinois	5.01	4.19
Maine	0.47	0.58
Massachusetts	2.91	2.37
Minnesota	1.46	1.58
Missouri	1.65	2.00
New York	7.51	6.63
Ohio	4.43	4.26
Oregon	0.98	1.24
Pennsylvania	4.96	4.59
South Dakota	0.26	0.25
Tennessee	1.93	2.07
Wisconsin	1.49	1.75
Total	47.71	43.66

n.a. = not available
SOURCE: A. C. Nielsen, Northbrook, Illinois, and calculations by the author.

a response by the national firms marketing products in these states. Many national firms may be located in the states that have pursued risk-warnings efforts, since the larger states are more likely to be affected. To the extent this occurs, many of the costs of warnings will be internalized within the state.

Table 3–6 summarizes the market shares for both drugs and grocery products for the states listed in table 2–1. Information is available on the national-market share represented in every case except for Hawaii. The fourteen states represented compose almost one-half of the U.S. market—48 percent of the market for drugs and 44 percent for grocery products. Such major states as California, New York, Illinois, Pennsylvania, and Ohio make up most of the large national market share accounted for by these fourteen states. If producers simply choose to ignore the regulations in these states and market their products elsewhere, they will forfeit a substantial portion of their national market. The extensive market representation is also a reflection of the magnitude of the impact of these warnings programs. They do not affect merely a small segment of the firm's activities, but in fact are national in scope.

It is noteworthy that the states that have adopted or are considering risk-labeling efforts have also taken initiatives against product advertising more generally.[5] Of the eleven leading states that have pursued advertising regulation, nine—California, Hawaii, Illinois, Massachusetts, Minnesota, Missouri, New York, Tennessee, and Wisconsin—are also included in the risk-labeling list in table 3–6. Only two states—Texas and Iowa—have pursued advertising regulations but not risk labeling. There is an 80 percent chance that a state that has adopted advertising regulations will also pursue risk labeling. If these policies were completely independent, the overlap would be just above 20 percent.

The difference between these efforts and a national regulation, however, is that the firms will face different and often conflicting requirements in the different states. To promote good nutrition, for example, federal law provides for the fortification of milk with vitamin A.[6] Because vitamin A at high levels is considered a reproductive toxicant, under typical state requirements the presence of vitamin A would trigger the warning requirement. In California, warnings are not required for milk because the listing of vitamin A (retinoic acid) defines it as a reproductive toxicant only when daily exposure exceeds 10,000 international units (IU) per day. This listing thus effectively exempts milk from the warning requirements. The fact that case-specific exemptions had to be granted for an obviously inappropriate warning highlights the fundamentally flawed nature of the scientific basis for the policy. Chemicals that may be less harmful than vitamin A will be required to bear a warning.

Even if we restrict our focus to the specific states that have adopted or are actively considering hazard-warnings programs, the extent of the market share represented is considerable. Table 3–7 presents three scenarios pertaining to adoption of the Proposition 65

---

[5]See J. Howard Beales and Timothy J. Muris, "State and Federal Regulation of National Advertising," Draft Monograph, American Enterprise Institute, 1992.

[6]See, for example, 21 Code of Federal Regulations 131.110.

TABLE 3–7
NATIONAL MARKET SHARE AFFECTED UNDER LABELING SCENARIOS
(percent)

State	Drugs	Grocery Products
Scenario 1		
California	14.65	12.15
Scenario 2		
California		
New York		
Ohio	26.59	23.04
Scenario 3		
California		
New York		
Ohio		
Massachusetts		
Illinois	34.51	29.60

SOURCE: Author.

type of measure. Under scenario 1, only California is represented. Even if California is the only state that adopts the warning, it comprises 15 percent of the national drug market and 12 percent of the national grocery-product market. Under scenario 2 in table 3–7, New York and Ohio are included as well. The addition of these two states brings the total national-market share represented by the hazard warnings to roughly one-fourth. In scenario 3, under which the total becomes five states through the addition of Massachusetts and Illinois, the total national-market share represented comes to roughly one-third.

Thus, even if only a few states adopt a Proposition 65 type of measure, the substantial market shares represented in each case will have a major effect on firms' product decisions. The character of these effects is explored below.

International Trade Repercussions

Although our primary focus is the adverse effect of fragmented markets for U.S. firms, state labeling regulations have international ramifications as well. The imposition of costs on firms that do business in several states similarly penalizes foreign firms that trade with the United States. The development of state labeling regulations will exacerbate international concerns over the accessibility of U.S. markets.

The European communities have expressed the following generic concerns, which have direct applicability to Proposition 65 types of measures:

> Other practices which cast doubt on the multilateral commitment of the United States include the inordinate time taken to bring U.S. legislation into conformity with GATT Panel rulings (the Customs User Fee is a good case in point), as well as the lukewarm attitude to International standard setting, its nonadherence to the relevant annexes of the Kyoto Convention on origin rules and its refusal to guarantee the compliance of its States with international obligations undertaken by the Federal government. . . . This concern has been heightened by the U.S. refusal, in both the Uruguay Round of GATT negotiations and in the ongoing talks in the OECD on the reinforcement of the National Treatment Instrument, to give a clear undertaking that its States will be bound by any agreement; up till now, the U.S. has only been prepared to offer a commitment on the basis of best endeavors.[7]

---

[7]Services of the Commission of the European Communities, *Report on the United States Trade Barriers and Unfair Practices, 1991*, March 15, 1991, pp. 5, 7.

4

Costs of Compliance, Warnings, and Reformulation

UNDER PROPOSITION 65 and related initiatives, the firm has the responsibility for ascertaining whether the product is above the risk threshold and for determining whether the listed chemical is in the product.

Costs of Testing and Litigation

Such tests are currently undertaken for products subject to pre-market approval by the FDA. Manufacturers routinely test for contaminants, both chemical and microbial, but they do not routinely test for each chemical likely to be listed under Proposition 65.

In addition to the testing costs, the firm has costs associated with litigation under Proposition 65. Under this act citizen suits are possible, as are suits by the state.

In large part because of the extent of exemptions, which may prove to be temporary, product-related litigation has not yet fully developed. Yet table 4–1 indicates that the litigation costs to firms will be significant.

The first set of enforcement actions listed in table 4–1 is sixty-day notices. These notices have been issued in the cases of seven types of products, including lantern mantles, cigars and pipes, Liquid Paper, toothpaste, spot remover, denture adhesives, and lead crystal.

In almost all cases, these notices have been followed by lawsuits alleging that individuals have been exposed to these risks without appropriate warning. Table 4–1 lists sixteen such lawsuits filed by public agencies.

For the most part, these cases against firms have been successful

44

TABLE 4–1

SUMMARY OF PRODUCT-RELATED ENFORCEMENT ACTIVITIES UNDER
PROPOSITION 65, AS OF JULY 1991

Product Type	Sixty-Day Notices
Lantern mantles	Notice by individual pertaining to thorium dioxide in ashes of camping lantern mantles
Cigars and pipes	Notice by Environmental Defense Fund (EDF) et al.; warning for tobacco products; warning given against twenty-five tobacco companies and eight retail chains
Liquid Paper	Notice of violation filed by EDF et al. against manufacturer and distributors of Liquid Paper for failure to warn of carcinogens
Toothpaste, mouthwash	Letters from attorney to Procter and Gamble and others claiming exposure to sodium saccharin in Crest toothpaste and Scope mouthwash
Spot remover, water repellent	Notice filed by EDF et al. for exposure to methylene chloride and perchloroethylene in spot remover and water repellent against Sears, K Mart, Standard Brands Paint Co., and other manufacturers and retailers
Denture adhesives	Citizens' notice for exposure to benzene filed against Cushion Grip and Brace denture adhesive
Lead crystal	Citizens' notice filed for lead exposure from crystal decanters and lead crystal baby bottles against Macy's, Steuben, Waterford, and others

(Table continues)

45

TABLE 4–1 (continued)

Enforcement Suit by Public Agency	Description
California v. Amvac Corp. and Bio-Strip	Alleges exposure to DDVP in bio-strip without a warning; case dismissed since there were fewer than ten employees at producing firm, and Amvac is therefore exempt
California v. H. W. Anderson Products and Anderson Products of California	Suit alleging no adequate warning for ethylene oxide exposure from desktop medical sterilizer device; litigation proceeding
California v. Baccarat, Inc., et al.	Suit alleging seventeen manufacturers and one retailer failed to warn of lead exposure from lead crystals; litigation proceeding
California v. Coleman	Suit against three companies selling lantern mantles (thorium dioxide exposure) without warning; settled for injunctive relief of $30,000, civil penalties, and on-package warnings requirement
California v. Dow brands	Suit claiming spot-remover exposure to perchloroethylene without warning; settled for $50,000 payment into Proposition 65 enforcement fund and reformulation of product
California v. Excell Products Corp.	Suit claiming no warning for paradichlorobenzene exposure from "Excell" brand moth crystals; penalty up to $27,000, reducible by consumer refunds
California v. Gillette Co.	Suit claiming Liquid Paper's failure to warn of carcinogens; Gillette paid $4,275,000 in civil penalties, $25,000 in costs and fees, and newspaper ad costs to inform public and offer safer formulation; reformulated product

TABLE 4–1 (continued)

Enforcement Suit by Public Agency	Description
California v. PPG	Suit claiming PPG must provide instruction to affix warning stickers prior to purchase and use certain warning language; settled on same day as filed, for $50,000 plus $25,000 costs
California v. Safeway	Suit claiming failure of tobacco companies to label cigar and pipe tobacco; settled for $750,000
California v. Sanitory	Suit claiming exposure without warning to paradichlorobenzene in Nursery Needs diaper-pail liner; settled and agreed to improve label and place newspaper ads offering consumers a refund
California v. Talson Corp.	Suit claiming exposure to methylene chloride in "Tai Strip" paint stripper; litigation proceeding
California v. Tobacco Manufacturers	See *California v. Safeway*
California v. Webb & Associates	Complaint for carcinogen warnings for mobile homes; partial settlement of $25,000 and permanent injunction
California v. Wirth International	Sequel to *California v. Gillette*; Wirth paid $17,500 to local drug education program, paid injunctive relief, and reformulated product
California v. Weilert Home Products, Inc., et al.	Exposure without warning to paradichlorobenzene in moth-control products, room fresheners, and household deodorizers; settled for improved warning and newspaper ads offering refund
California v. Wite Out Co.	Sequel to *California v. Gillette*; settled for $50,000, injunctive relief, product reformulation, and warning to consumers about old formulation

(Table continues)

47

TABLE 4–1 (continued)

Suit against State Agencies or Officials	Description
CURL v. Allenby	Complaint seeking to declare provisions of Proposition 65 pertaining to food and food packaging null and void because of preexemption by federal law, unconstitutional burden on interstate commerce, and violation of due-process clause of the U.S. Constitution; motion not granted; case on hold
D-Con v. Allenby	Petition to declare Proposition 65 labeling requirements for insecticides preempted by FIFRA; petition denied
Chemical Specialty Manufacturer's Assn. v. California Health and Welfare Agency	Complaint alleging Proposition 65 warning requirements preempted by FIFRA, FHSA, and Federal OSHA; summary judgment in favor of defendants
AFL-CIO v. Deukmejian (I)	Petition to obtain list of 200 additional chemicals as "known to the state . . . [to be carginogenic]"; appellate decision upheld inclusion of IARC, NRC, NTP, and OSHA carcinogens
AFL-CIO v. Deukmejian (II)	Complaint challenging regulatory exemption of food, drug, and cosmetic products; decision voiding exemption under appeal
AFL-CIO v. Deukmejian (III)	Complaint petitioning state to designate "authoritative bodies"; settled; EPA recognized as an authoritative body
Nicolle-Wagner v. Deukmejian	Complaint to list vitamin A as reproductive toxicant dismissed, since science advisory panel will consider
Nicolle-Wagner v. Deukmejian	Complaint challenged "naturally occurring" exemption; exemption upheld
I.C.C. v. Van DeKamp	Ingredient Communication Council sought declaration that 1-800 system is "clear and reasonable"; decision against system under appeal

SOURCE: Author.

and have led to out-of-court settlements. The total penalties paid thus far have been in excess of $1.3 million; the largest penalty has been $750,000, paid by the tobacco companies for not labeling cigar and pipe tobacco a carcinogen.

The firms in these cases have also incurred other costs. The typical settlement requires that the company issue a public notice of a product recall, whereby they agree to reimburse consumers for the cost of the product. In addition the company must advertise in newspapers to alert consumers to this possibility. All future versions of the product must either be labeled or reformulated. The reformulation option has been selected by firms that sell spot remover, Liquid Paper, and related products such as Wite Out.

Some of the cases listed in table 4–1 are still pending, so additional penalties, reformulations, and other actions by firms may be generated by these enforcement activities.

The last section of enforcement actions listed in table 4–1 consists of suits against state agencies and officials, largely to clarify the intent or limit the scope of Proposition 65. The two major suits by industry are the suits in *CURL v. Allenby*, in which the industry unsuccessfully sought to have Proposition 65 food-and-drug packaging requirements declared null and void because of federal preemption. The industry's attempt in *I.C.C. v. Van DeKamp* to have the toll-free-number system approved as an acceptable warning under Proposition 65 was not successful, although this decision is under appeal.

The most important of the other suits against the states listed in table 4–1 is *AFL-CIO v. Deukmejian II*. The AFL-CIO and several environmental groups challenged the regulatory exemption from Proposition 65 that had been given to food, drug, and cosmetic products. The court voided the exemption, although this case is currently on appeal. Should this decision be upheld, the scope of Proposition 65 would be greatly extended.

In contrast, the challenge of the exemption for "naturally occurring" carcinogens in *Nicolle Wagner v. Deukmejian* was not successful. This exemption was upheld so that firms need not provide warnings for chemicals that occur naturally in foods if they are at background levels.

From the standpoint of risk communication, an exemption for naturally occurring carcinogens cannot be justified. Consumers are concerned justifiably with all risks, whether they occur naturally or

49

are man-made. But the exemption for naturally occurring carcinogens was based largely on practical considerations. To ease the testing burden on firms, California regulators responsible for the implementation of Proposition 65 chose to exclude naturally occurring carcinogens from consideration. This exemption does not mean that firms are free to market peanuts with high levels of aflatoxin. The presence of carcinogens must be naturally occurring, assuming that the firm has exercised appropriate levels of care with respect to the handling and processing of the food product. High levels of aflatoxin in peanuts consequently would not be permissible under this exemption.

Reformulation Costs

As indicated above, the costs associated with on-product labels are likely to be substantial. In practice, however, it is unlikely that use of on-product labels would become widespread for food-and-drug products with risk levels in excess of the Proposition 65 threshold: companies would prefer to reformulate the product, if at all possible. Possibly the risk label will stigmatize the product not only in that state but in others as well. As the analysis of Proposition 65 in chapter 5 indicates, the required wording implies a substantial risk—one that dwarfs the actual risk likely to be posed by the product. Most companies will be reluctant to market a food or pharmaceutical product with such a warning for two reasons.

First, the strong content of the warning would in all likelihood depress consumer demand within that state. Second, adverse ramifications would follow in other states as well. The company would have difficulty in marketing a product in other states if that product had a warning alerting consumers to the cancer risk in California. Should consumers become aware of this warning, it would stigmatize the product. Moreover, consumers would begin to distrust the honesty of the company and its other products if it provided important risk information to consumers in some states and not others. As a result, firms would prefer to withdraw the food or drug product altogether rather than put a label on it.

The costs of withdrawing a product because of an ingredient that must be removed can be substantial. Replacing the ingredient may take substantial time, because of the needs both to reformulate the product and to incorporate the new ingredients in the production process.

Previous experience with reformulations and product recalls suggests that the costs to manufacturers may be substantial. The Perrier experience in 1990 illustrates the problems entailed in removing an ingredient—in this case, trace elements of benzene. The costs of the recall were estimated to be $149 million.[1] Only a fraction of this amount was attributable to the cost of returning the suspect bottles. The greater share consisted of the lost sales and possibly permanent stigmatization of the product. Perrier sales in 1991 remained below the levels that prevailed before the benzene controversy, and the costs of the ingredient removal are not yet fully known.[2]

The extent of these costs is also suggested by experience after the government's ban on the use of cyclamate sweeteners in diet foods.[3] After the government announced the cyclamate ban on October 18, 1969, sales of food products containing cyclamates plummeted. In the initial four-week period following the announcement, sales of diet foods were down by 50 percent from the previous year. Even twenty weeks after the announcement, sales of all diet foods were down by 42–49 percent.

The extent of these longer-run impacts varied within different diet-food categories. Some diet foods, including canned fruit and diet desserts, lost more than half their sales in major national markets. Substantial losses of between one-third and one-half of the pre-ban market share were experienced by diet sweeteners, canned vegetables, diet jams and jellies, and measured-portion diet meals. The least affected category was diet salad dressings, with losses of only about one-fifth of the market, because cyclamates play a smaller role

---

[1]*New York Times*, June 30, 1990.

[2]Some might suggest that the drop in Perrier sales reflects a return to rationality. Once consumers realized that high-priced European waters did not offer clearly superior health benefits over alternative and less expensive beverages, such as domestic tap water or distilled water, the demand for Perrier may have better reflected its economic value to informed consumers. The key aspect of this event is that there was a strong market response, not that this response was irrational.

[3]The cyclamate statistics are based on studies of seven major national markets by selling areas. Marketing, Inc., "The Cyclamate Ban: Its Effect upon Sales of Selected Diet Foods," January 20, 1970.

in these products. Although the effect of a reformulation caused by Proposition 65 listing could be more or less than the cyclamate experience, companies could lose a substantial share of their affected market.[4]

One means of avoiding the warning is to reformulate the product. It is impossible to predict the costs of reformulation without knowing the character of the chemical and its importance to the product. Some chemical ingredients are fundamental to the product; others play a minor role in either the taste or the appearance of the product. Since companies do not yet have complete knowledge of the presence of all chemicals likely to be listed under Proposition 65 or of the extent to which compliance is likely to be a problem, they cannot predict what reformulation costs will be.

The Liquid Paper experience represents a best-case scenario. Gillette had already developed an alternative formulation of the product. After receiving notice that Liquid Paper violated California's Proposition 65, the company brought to the market a substitute formulation in compliance with the standard, without any warning.

This favorable situation will not hold generally. Companies do not routinely develop alternative formulations of their products. When they do, moreover, the objective has not been compliance with a potential Proposition 65 requirement. Substantial research and product-development costs would therefore be entailed in developing such alternative reformulations. And once these products have been developed, the company would have to test-market different varieties of them to see which change in the product would meet with the greatest consumer acceptance. Demand for these new formulations might also be lower.

A less extreme reformulation is seen in efforts to remove BHA from products. Some companies have already begun to reformulate products by removing this chemical ingredient, which helps to preserve freshness. The main cost arises from shortened shelf life of products. In this case, the product's attributes remain virtually intact, but an economic cost to both consumers and manufacturers results from the shorter period of sale and shorter period of consumer

---

[4]There will, of course, be some substitution of other goods. These greater sales, however, may not benefit the company affected by the reformulation. Moreover, these sales do not imply that the adjustment costs associated with reformulation are small.

use. Balanced against these costs are the possible health benefits to consumers.

Should a firm be subject to a product recall as part of this reformulation effort, the firm would be forced to withdraw its product from the stores. Companies have become efficient in undertaking such withdrawals, particularly in the present era of Stock Keeping Unit (SKU) codes stamped on products. As a result, the primary cost of the recall would not be much greater than the total value of the goods being sold. For perishable commodities, it would be more costly to withdraw the product from the stores and ship it to another state than to destroy it. The recall costs in such instances would be tantamount to the value of the goods.

Labeling and Distribution Costs

In cases where firms choose to provide the warning indicated by the regulation rather than to reformulate the product, a complex set of effects would influence the cost of the product to the consumer. Before considering the specific level of these costs, we should look at how products are currently produced and distributed.

Most products marketed nationally are produced in one or more regional locations that serve a large number of states. These products are generally produced for a national market, not for individual states. Perhaps the main exception is the soft-drink market, in which national brands such as Coke and Pepsi are produced regionally by local bottlers. The soft-drink industry is better able to adapt to state-specific requirements, such as beverage-container recycling laws, because soft drinks produced in Atlanta are not sold in Los Angeles. Rather, Los Angeles is served by a California bottler, which can alter labels for that market.

The effect of Proposition 65 and related measures would require that firms produce labels for different products sold in different states. Multiple formulations of the product might also affect the number of labels to be produced.

The site of the label application is likely to be the point of manufacture. Because the firm then loses control of the product, there is no guarantee that the label would remain on the product. Since the producing firm has responsibility for providing the warning under California's Proposition 65 and the other initiatives, it would be unlikely to relinquish control over this compliance decision.

Although there are notable exceptions, such as the delivery of bakery and snack-food products by company trucks, most nationally marketed grocery and drug products are sold to wholesalers that distribute the product. To ensure appropriate targeting of markets, products would have to be segregated in the distribution system. In all likelihood, warehousing would increase within the states requiring warnings, thus creating additional employment. Moreover, firms would want to have greater control over this process than they now have.

The placement of warning labels on the containers is likely to be required at the point of manufacture, since these warnings would probably have to be part of the label graphics as opposed to supplementary stickers. And for most products, the logistics of adding a sticker on a decentralized basis are likely to be considerably greater than they were for cigarettes. Cigarette-tax stamps can be applied at the state level without inordinate costs because the stamp is the same for all brands. This would clearly not be the case for consumer products under Proposition 65, which require labels only if they do not meet the risk threshold.

The net effect of these labeling changes would be an increase in the number of items handled in the product-manufacturing stage, thus decreasing the sales volume of any particular item. Since there are economies of scale in manufacturing, costs would increase, wholly apart from the fixed costs associated with changing over to different items.

Inventories would also have to increase because of the fragmentation of product lines. Greater inventories would be required, both for finished products and for the labels themselves. This is a basic consequence of queuing theory. Inventory control would require that the stocks increase with the number of items separately labeled. As a rule of thumb, the increase would be proportional to the square root of the number of items. Thus, if a firm were to manufacture products with four different labels, the required inventory would have to double. There would also be the risk of increased spoilage as the inventories became increasingly fragmented. These inventories would have to be increased not only at the point of manufacture but also downstream.

In many instances the labeling change would affect the cost of

54

not only the labeling but also the packaging, because packages such as breakfast cereals are often manufactured at the same time as they are printed. Thus the fragmentation of the production process would result in a loss of scale economies and in increased packaging costs.

Manufacturing costs would also rise. Producing special formulations of a product for different states not only entails direct costs but also fragments the production of the product, forfeiting the economies of scale that are possible for large production runs.

Compliance management costs would increase. The company would have to ensure that inventories reached the right state. Since little tracking of this type takes place at present for most products, increased monitoring of the state in which the product was sold would entail a substantial change in the distribution system.

Transportation costs would rise. As shipping lots became fragmented for targeted distribution, higher transportation costs would accrue from the labeling change.

Warehouse handling costs would increase for analogous reasons, as warehouses handle smaller lots of the product. If warehouse capacity had to be expanded capital costs would be incurred.

All these changes would create entry barriers for states. If a state has a specific labeling regulation, as has California, it would be more costly for out-of-state firms to enter and sell their products. The loss of competition would lead to increased consumer prices.

The consequences of the labeling requirements depend in part on whether the product is produced nationally or locally. Table 4–2 provides a breakdown of the distribution of national retail sales of food products. Such foods as produce and fresh fish are locally produced and distributed. But measured in dollar volume of retail sales, almost half of all food products are nationally or regionally produced and distributed. This fraction is even higher for pharmaceutical products.

Even where the product is produced locally, there would be many of the costs mentioned earlier. Packages would have to be redesigned and new labels applied. It has been estimated, for example, that the cost in California to the local bottlers of Coca-Cola and Pepsi-Cola for redesigning their cans for carbonated beverages would be $200,000 to $300,000.[5] This estimate was based on the

---

[5]SRI International, "The Effects on the Food Industry of the Labeling Requirements

TABLE 4–2
DISTRIBUTION OF NATIONAL RETAIL SALES OF FOOD PRODUCTS
ANALYZED, 1986

Food Products	Value of Retail Sales ($billions)	Percentage of Total
Locally produced and distributed products		
Produce and fresh fish	40.4	21
Packaged goods (except water and carbonated beverages)	53.5	28
Water and carbonated beverages in bottles	10.4	5
Carbonated beverages in cans	1.7	1
Subtotal	106.0	55
Nationally or regionally produced and distributed products	87.7	45
Total	193.7	100

SOURCES: SRI (Stanford Research Institute) International and *Supermarket Business*, September 1987.

carbonated-beverage industry's experience in complying with the California Beverage Container Recycling and Litter Reduction Act of 1986.

The costs of adding a label to other kinds of products is likely to be substantial as well. Consider, for example, the estimates by General Foods.[6] The firm must first acquire the chemical analysis of its product, to identify the listed chemicals and their concentrations. It must then ascertain whether the concentration is in compliance with the risk thresholds—a difficult process, since California has specified few chemical exposure amounts corresponding to the risk threshold. The company must assume responsibility for this judg-

in the Safe Drinking Water and Toxic Enforcement Act of 1986," Final Report, February 1988.

[6]These estimates are based on a speech at the 1990 IFT annual meeting by K. Raneri, General Foods Technical Center at Anaheim, California, June 18, 1990.

TABLE 4–3
ESTIMATED INCREASES IN TRANSPORTATION AND DISTRIBUTION COSTS
FROM LABELING A PRODUCT THAT COSTS $.50, 1990

Cost Element	Current Cost (dollars)	Percent Increase	Dollar Increase
Transportation	.03259	10 (because of fragmented parcels)	.003259
Plant warehousing	.00379	40	.001516
Field warehousing	.00603	20	.001206
Inventory	.01116	33⅓₅	.00372
Total	.05357	18	.009701

SOURCE: Arthur D. Little, "The Impact of Multi-State Labeling Requirements on Grocery Logistics and Food Costs," July 5, 1990.

ment. This cost would range from $3,000 to $5,000 per product, under a best-case scenario. If the firm chose to print the labels directly on containers the cost would be $5,000 to $10,000; changing labels applied to containers would cost about $1,000.

Implementing this labeling change would be costly. Labels printed on special equipment are difficult to alter. The cost of changing a line of twelve currently labeled products is estimated to be $160,000, or more than $13,000 per product. In addition, the package might have to be redesigned to accommodate the labeling information, leading to a cost of $10,000 to $50,000 per package.

If all products at General Foods were required to bear such a label, the labeling costs would range from $20 million to $30 million. If 10 percent of the products were affected, the costs would be roughly $2 million to $3 million. Thus the ultimate scope of the labeling regulation will determine costs. At present, the extent of coverage of Proposition 65 and related measures is unclear.

Even after the labels have been applied to the product, the firm must incur additional costs related to transportation and distribution. Table 4–3 summarizes cost estimates for these categories, where illustrative calculations are presented for a hypothetical consumer product that has a manufacturing cost of $.50 and a current retail price of $1.00. These estimates may be low since they neglect capital costs, such as new labeling machinery and increased warehouse capacity.

Table 4–3 focuses on the transportation and distribution costs only, which account for roughly a nickel of the cost of this hypothetical product. As a result of the fragmented production, transportation costs per $.50 of product costs would rise from $.03 by roughly 10 percent. Planned warehousing would increase by 40 percent and field warehousing by 20 percent. In addition there would be a one-third increase in inventory costs. Based on a scenario in which one assumes that companies must produce labels in response to ten labeling regulations, transportation costs would rise by 1.94 percent.

For other scenarios we can adjust these cost increases appropriately. For scenario 3 outlined above, in which five states are affected rather than the ten assumed for this calculation, the added transportation and distribution cost would be roughly half this estimate, or 1 percent of total costs, if costs are proportional to the number of regulations. If the relationship is not proportional but varies with the square root of the number of labels produced, as in classic inventory theory, then the cost would be approximately 70 percent of this estimate, or 1.4 percent of the manufacturer's direct product and logistic costs.

Since the product costs make up roughly half the purchase price to consumers, a ten-state labeling regulation would increase consumer costs by approximately 1 percent, and a five-state regulation would increase these costs by about 0.7 percent.

The national value of these costs is substantial. Consider the food-product component based on the data in table 4–2. The total value of retail sales of food products sold nationally in 1991 dollars is approximately $100 billion. One percent of this amount is $1 billion. Under the five-state labeling scenario, approximately $700 million in transportation and distribution costs would be imposed if all products received the label. If only one out of fourteen products were labeled, the annual cost associated with labeling and distribution would be $50 million.

These cost estimates, while substantial, are only partial. They were based on early, selected segments of the cost impacts. As the discussion of product-risk labeling indicates, the ramifications of the warning requirements go beyond the costs of warehousing and isolated reformulation. If a product is reformulated, for example, its properties and marketing strategy may be affected.

The impact of these costs may differ significantly by firm size.

Other variables being equal, larger firms will be better able to deal with market fragmentation because of their greater economies of scale. Firms with more distribution centers, such as producers of soft drinks and snack foods, will be less affected than firms with fewer such centers.

The calculation of costs provided above derives from a national perspective. It is true, of course, that some costs will be shifted to California consumers. A cost distribution will thus be shared by consumers in California, consumers in the rest of the country, and companies. The distribution is complex and hinges on the supply-and-demand elasticities involved.[7]

The calculations prepared here do not distinguish costs borne by California residents from those imposed on the rest of the country, for several reasons. First, thus far our cost estimates are largely suggestive. We know the costs are likely to be significant, but we do not know their exact level or the division between labeling costs and reformulation costs. Until we know which option a company will choose—whether to withdraw a product, reformulate it, or label it—it is impossible to calculate the exact cost-shift. If the company reformulates the product nationally, all costs will be shared nationally.

Second, the cost-shift cannot be predicted without knowing the benefits the consumers will place on the information. How will the risk information provided by California's Proposition 65 and related measures affect the attractiveness of products to consumers? At face value the warnings will depress the attractiveness of products, so demand will shift downward considerably. Until we know how far this shift will go, we cannot determine the cost-allocation. If reaction to a warning is so strong that California residents never buy any product bearing it, clearly they will bear no cost-shift.

The third and perhaps most important reason for not analyzing the distribution to California residents is that the standard procedure for all regulatory analyses reviewed by the federal government is to

---

[7]Calculations that provide suggestive estimates of the cost-shifting are provided in the report by Lexecon, "An Economic Analysis of the Costs of Proposition 65 That Will Be Imposed on Out-of-State Producers," November 15, 1988. Lexecon estimates that 35–70 percent of the costs will not be shifted to California consumers. For different assumptions, such as a supply elasticity of two, 10 percent of the costs will be shifted out of state.

consider national costs, not to net out costs to particular groups. When the U.S. Department of Transportation and the Office of Management and Budget assess the merits of automobile safety regulation, for example, they do not divide costs into those borne by purchasers of automobiles and those borne by producers. Rather the emphasis is on the national effects, to determine whether these policies are attractive for the nation as a whole. Similarly, when evaluating acid-rain policies that disproportionately benefit the northeastern section of the United States, the EPA did not calculate the cost to the parts of the country that will not benefit from the environmental improvements. Regional cost distributions are not even analyzed.

Similarly, the issue here is whether national action is desirable with respect to food-and-drug product labeling. Is the policy warranted, given the benefits and the costs to the entire country, not simply the benefits and costs to those states not involved in the warnings efforts? To maintain consistency with the other regulatory analyses performed at the federal level and with the context of the decision to which this study relates—a national decision—my focus has been on national costs and benefits.

5

Do Consumers Benefit from Informational Costs?

FIRMS WILL NOT BE the only parties to bear costs from product-risk labeling. If these efforts are not well designed, consumers may pay a net cost because of alarmism.

Informational Costs

Ideally, risk-communication efforts should provide net benefits to consumers, the major benefit being improved decision making made possible by superior information. But state risk-communication efforts may well distort decision making. The wording and the nature of the warning efforts can be entirely disproportionate to the actual level of the risks. Thus consumers and firms will face the costs of an inappropriately designed warnings effort.

Consider the safe-harbor warning language about cancer used by California: "WARNING: This product contains a chemical known to the state of California to cause cancer." Several attributes can be evaluated using insights from scientific literature on sound risk communication.[1] The warning begins with the human-hazard signal word "warning" and is followed by a succinct fourteen-word message that links the product to cancer.

Consider first the human-hazard signal word. In the hierarchy of such terms, "danger" is the most severe, "warning" ranks second, and "caution" third. For small risks one might abandon such a signal

---

[1]For a succinct review of these scientific principles, see chapter 7 of W. Kip Viscusi, *Reforming Products Liability* (Cambridge: Harvard University Press, 1991). More generally, see W. Kip Viscusi and Wesley A. Magat, *Learning About Risk: Consumer and Worker Responses to Hazard Information* (Cambridge: Harvard University Press, 1987).

TABLE 5-1
WARNING CONTENT SUMMARIES, 1977 AND 1982

Product Warning Group	Warning Content
Proposition 65—food	WARNING: This product contains a chemical known to the state of California to cause cancer.[a]
Proposition 65—restaurants	WARNING: Chemicals known to the state of California to cause cancer or birth defects or other reproductive harm may be present in foods or beverages served here.[b]
Proposition 65—occupational or environmental	WARNING: This area contains a chemical known to the state of California to cause cancer.[c]
Saccharin	USE OF THIS PRODUCT MAY BE HAZARDOUS TO YOUR HEALTH. THIS PRODUCT CONTAINS SACCHARIN WHICH HAS BEEN DETERMINED TO CAUSE CANCER IN LABORATORY ANIMALS.[d]
Cigarette warning, 1965	Caution: Cigarette Smoking May Be Hazardous to Your Health.[e]
Cigarette warning, 1969	Warning: The Surgeon General Has Determined That Cigarette Smoking Is Dangerous To Your Health.[f]

Cigarette warning, 1984   • SURGEON GENERAL'S WARNING: Smoking Causes Lung Cancer, Heart Disease, Emphysema, and May Complicate Pregnancy.[g]
         • SURGEON GENERAL'S WARNING: Quitting Smoking Now Greatly Reduces Serious Risks to Your Health.[h]
         • SURGEON GENERAL'S WARNING: Smoking by Pregnant Women May Result in Fetal Injury, Premature Birth, and Low Birth Weight.[i]
         • SURGEON GENERAL'S WARNING: Cigarette Smoke Contains Carbon Monoxide.[j]

a. Codified at California Administrative Code tit. 22, § 12601(b) (4) (A).
b. Ibid., § 12601(b) (4) (C).
c. Ibid., § 12601(c) (3) (A).
d. Saccharin Study and Labeling Act, November 1977.
e. 15 U.S.Code §§ 1331–1341 (1982).
f. Ibid.
g. Ibid.
h. Ibid.
i. Ibid.
j. Ibid.
SOURCE: Author.

altogether and simply provide the warning message. Use of the all upper-cased "WARNING" inappropriately alerts consumers to the presence of a substantial risk. "DANGER" suggests that the risk is a more certain consequence. "CAUTION" would be appropriate for health risks other than cancer.

The warning that follows the signal word is also strong. It links the product to a risk of cancer—a word that evokes substantial negative response. The warning does not indicate that this potential link is probabilistic, but rather that the product contains something that *causes* cancer. A consumer reading the warning might conclude the risk is considerable, whereas it may be only a 1/100,000 lifetime risk, or a 1/7,000,000 risk from annual consumption. Such risks are dwarfed by less rare events, such as the probability of being struck by lightning. Indeed, some scientists estimate that the probability the consumer will be killed by an asteroid impact—the doomsday rock—is 1,000 times greater than the risk being addressed by Proposition 65. In view of the low magnitude of the risk, if a product carries a warning at all, it should be commensurately low.

Table 5–1 compares the content of the California warnings with nationally mandated warnings for saccharin and cigarettes. The California wording is strong compared with these other warnings. The risk-assessment procedures that will be used to determine whether a product passes the risk threshold in California have been used in other contexts as well. These procedures indicate that exposure to saccharin poses an individual lifetime risk of cancer of 1/2,500.[2] The estimated lifetime mortality risk from cigarette smoking is well over 1/10, or 10,000 times greater than the risk threshold in California.[3]

Comparison of the warnings would not indicate that such a difference exists. Although the carcinogen warning in California indicates a definite link, in the case of saccharin we know only that it has been linked to cancer in laboratory animals, not humans. Similarly, the early warnings for cigarettes indicated that smoking "may be hazardous"; this was strengthened in 1969 to read "is

---

[2]See C. Travis et al., "Cancer Risk Management: A Review of 132 Federal Regulatory Decisions," *Environmental Science Technology*, vol. 21 (1987), pp. 415–20.

[3]See W. Kip Viscusi, *Smoking: Making the Risky Decision* (New York: Oxford University Press, 1992).

hazardous." But more definite linkage, with the phrasing "smoking may cause . . . ," did not occur until 1984.

California's Proposition 65 warning seems patterned directly on the first of the cigarette warnings adopted in 1984. But using an existing warning as a reference point is particularly inappropriate, because we are attempting to convey information regarding a risk much smaller than that of cigarettes. A difference of a factor of 10,000 should distinguish a risk one can reasonably ignore from one of major concern.

Northwestern University Test Sample

The ultimate test of the efficacy of the warning as a risk-communication device hinges on the degree to which consumers can process the information reliably and form accurate risk judgments. To test whether consumers would process California's Proposition 65 wording accurately, I distributed a questionnaire to ninety-nine adult participants in a continuing-education course at Northwestern University during the fall of 1987.[4] The first task given them was to compare the California warning (with "California" replaced by "Illinois") to other warnings for implied risk level. These results are reported in table 5–2.

The first of the reference warnings listed is for saccharin products. More than half the sample views the warning as implying a risk lower than that of the Proposition 65 warning, although the risk level involved is forty times greater than the Proposition 65 risk threshold. The remainder of the sample is equally divided between believing that saccharin is more risky or equally risky, compared with products bearing the Proposition 65 warning.

The second warning listed in table 5–2 is an amended version of the 1969 cigarette warning, except that the surgeon general has been replaced by the state of Illinois to establish comparability with the variant of the Proposition 65 warning. In this case, half the consumers tested believed the variant of the 1969 cigarette warning was roughly comparable in severity to the Proposition 65 warning. The next largest group—more than one-third of all respondents—

---

[4]For a fuller description of this study, see W. Kip Viscusi, "Predicting the Effect of Food Cancer Risk Warnings on Consumers," *Food Drug Cosmetic Law Journal*, vol. 43 (1988), pp. 283–307.

TABLE 5–2

COMPARISON OF PROPOSITION 65 WARNING WITH OTHER WARNINGS,
1987 SURVEY

Hazard Warning	Fraction Who Regard Other as Less Risky	Fraction Who Regard Other as More Risky	Fraction Who Regard Other as Equal in Risk
Use of this product may be hazardous to your health. This product contains a chemical that has been determined to cause cancer in laboratory animals.	.56	.26	.18
Warning: The state of Illinois has determined that this product is dangerous to your health.	.36	.16	.48
Caution: Use of this product may be hazardous to your health.	.14	.17	.69

NOTE: The wording of Proposition 65 is as follows: "Warning: The state of California has determined that this product is dangerous to your health."
SOURCE: W. Kip Viscusi, "Predicting the Effect of Food Cancer Risk Warnings on Consumers," *Food Drug Cosmetic Law Journal*, vol. 43 (1988).

believed this modified 1969 cigarette warning implied a lower risk than did the California Proposition 65 warning.

The final warning tested in table 5–2 gives the exact wording of the 1965 cigarette warning. Perhaps in part because consumers remembered this warning language and linked it to cigarettes, they viewed this one as stronger than the variant of the 1969 cigarette warning. The great majority of consumers viewed the 1965 cigarette warning wording as implying a risk tantamount to that implied by the Proposition 65 warning.

TABLE 5–3
CONSUMERS' ESTIMATES OF DANGER FROM PROPOSITION 65 WARNING,
1987 SURVEY

Risk Range	Fraction Who Put Product in Range	Score within Range on a 10-point scale
Zero Risk–one 12-ounce saccharin cola	.21	4.86
One Saccharin–one pack of cigarettes	.44	4.27
One pack of cigarettes–five packs of cigarettes	.35	2.25

SOURCE: Author.

The next test was to ask the consumers to rate the riskiness of a breakfast cereal containing the Proposition 65 warning relative to other risks, using linear scales. Table 5–3 summarizes the risk ranges that consumers confronted. I first asked the respondents to say which of the three ranges was most appropriate for cereal bearing a Proposition 65 warning. Was the product less risky than a twelve-ounce saccharin cola; between a twelve-ounce saccharin cola and one pack of cigarettes; or between one and five packs of cigarettes? The most frequent response—44 percent of the sample—believed that cereal bearing a Proposition 65 warning was between a saccharin cola and one pack of cigarettes in terms of its riskiness. Strikingly, more than one-third of the sample believed the product risk fell between one and five packs of cigarettes in riskiness.

I then asked consumers to rate from one to ten where the product fell within the risk range they selected. Among those who selected the first range—less than a twelve-ounce saccharin cola—the average viewed the product as roughly half as risky as this drink. For those who believed the product was between a twelve-ounce saccharin cola and a pack of cigarettes, the average response rated the risk as equivalent to .4 packs of cigarettes. For those who placed the risk between one and five packs of cigarettes, the average response rated the risk as equivalent to two packs of cigarettes.

One can also combine the response in table 5–3 to establish the total cigarette-pack equivalent of these ratings. If we treat all the responses of the first range as viewing the risks posed to be zero, then the sample believes that cereal with a Proposition 65 warning poses the same risk as .58 packs of cigarettes. Based on the surgeon general's estimates of the risks posed by cigarettes, this implies an associated risk above 1/10, or 10,000 times greater than the risk threshold for California Proposition 65. That a breakfast cereal bearing a Proposition 65 warning should be equated with cigarettes, a recognized substantial hazard, suggests that the warnings effort is fundamentally misguided.

To test the sensitivity of the responses to the wording of the warning question, I also asked the respondents how many of 11 million Illinois residents would develop cancer from daily lifetime consumption of cereal that bore a Proposition 65 warning. The sample indicated that on average they expected 1,316,729 deaths. These responses indicate a lifetime cancer risk of .12, which is consistent with their responses to the risk-scale questions.

Clearly, California's Proposition 65 wording indicates to consumers an extremely large risk, not a trace-carcinogenic risk or speculative reproductive hazard. This inappropriate warning will lead to substantial costs for mistaken decisions. Consumers will forgo consumption of products that are not excessively risky, given their own preferences and attitudes toward risk. Their decisions will be distorted, as they devote increasing concern to minimal risks and ignore the fundamental ones posed by inadequate diet.

One can only speculate how this situation developed. Significantly, the warning message was never tested with groups of consumers to allow California to ascertain what level of risk was being conveyed. Had the government undertaken such a test, it would have determined that the warning language was entirely inappropriate to the risk involved.

Even if the government had undertaken such a test or had tried different language, it probably would have discovered the difficulty of communicating a low probability. The risk threshold associated with the California warning is minimal, well below the risks typically conveyed through hazard warnings. Moreover, annual risks of 1/7,000,000 lie outside our normal realm of risk experience. By comparison, the average worker faces an annual fatality risk of 1/10,000, and the average American faces a risk of being killed in an aviation accident in any given year of 1/100,000. Even the risk of being struck by lightning exceeds the risk threshold for California's Proposition 65.

Upon completion of the survey, the Illinois respondents were told about the magnitude of the risk in relation to other hazards, such as being struck by lightning. Their reaction was that the labels were yet another example of inexplicable governmental actions. This response suggests that the background of the labeling policy, provided by the government and by the media, may be influential. The number of products affected by the warning and consumers' prior beliefs about product safety will also affect how warnings are viewed. If a large percentage of products receive a warning, consumers will attach a lower risk to the warning than if only very dangerous products are labeled. Clearly, the warnings are not particularly instructive in conveying the risks to which they pertain.

Unfortunately, it is difficult to change the wording of a warning to convey a very low level of risk. The act of placing a warning on a product stamps it as risky. The product then joins the class of products bearing warnings, including hazardous household chemicals and cigarettes. Risk communication methods that are more commensurate with low levels of risk would be more accurate and appropriate.

6

Conclusion

ALTHOUGH CALIFORNIA VOTERS passed Proposition 65 in 1986, the effects of this initiative have not been substantial or widespread. Visitors to California supermarkets and drugstores will find evidence of this regulation to be relatively minor.

One should not, however, dismiss this risk-labeling effort as inconsequential. The full effect of Proposition 65 will become apparent if the temporary exemption given to products regulated by the FDA is removed. It will be removed, unless a lower-court ruling is reversed. In the long run, the main cost will not be that of the warning labels: rather, it will be expenditures made by firms.

The chief costs likely to be affected are those of testing products, of reformulating products with listed chemicals, and of segregating products with state-specific warnings. There is substantial uncertainty about these costs, since the ultimate product coverage is not yet known and, for reproductive toxicants, will not be known for years or even decades.

Firms also face substantial uncertainty about which states will adopt warnings programs and what inconsistencies will arise among them. The increasing prevalence of Proposition 65 types of initiatives suggests that the warnings experiment will not be limited to California but will involve many states, composing a substantial share of the national market. As the market becomes fragmented, the costs of complying with the different warnings requirements will increase. This fragmentation will create entry barriers for out-of-state firms and will deter international competition.

In view of these costs, the economic question to ask is, Will these policies provide benefits commensurate with the burdens they impose? Unfortunately, the warnings effort is likely to be harmful to consumers. The character and the mere placement of an on-product warning are out of proportion to the underlying risk. The primary risk-communication problem is that decentralized warnings efforts distort the warnings vocabulary mandated by Congress and federal regulatory agencies.

That various state warnings proposals are inappropriate does not necessarily imply that all possible warnings systems are undesirable. The California system and other state proposals have two main deficiencies. First, using a state-based warnings policy fragments the market and potentially leads to inconsistent warnings approaches. By adopting a uniform federal warnings system, the deficiencies could be eliminated.

The second shortcoming is that the state efforts have not been well thought out. The warnings language is disproportionate to the trace cancer and reproductive risks involved. The resulting system would not inform but would rather needlessly alarm consumers.

These difficulties are not insurmountable. The objective, however, is not to formulate a warnings system closely analogous to that for cigarettes. The assessed risk posed by cigarettes is many orders of magnitude larger than the hazards likely to be posed by the food-and-drug products considered under these state measures. The mode and language of warning should be formulated to reflect these differences.

The general principle underlying Proposition 65 and related measures—that providing additional information serves a constructive role—appears to be a sound one. Product-ingredient bans affect the more severe risks, and the existing warnings efforts for tobacco, alcohol, and saccharin are limited to only a few select products. Existing warnings are in place for such targeted products as pesticides, but no across-the-board federal warnings system ensures inclusive coverage of potentially risky products. For products that are not too risky to be marketed yet contain some risk that should be told to consumers, intermediate policy solutions such as warnings can play an important role.

Warnings also offer considerably more flexibility than do product bans. With a warnings system, consumers who are most sensitive to particular risks can reflect their preferences in consumption choices. In the absence of warnings to inform consumers, the opportunities for making appropriate risk trade-offs and efficient consumption decisions will be limited.

The first prerequisite for any sound risk-communication system

71

is that it be based on an honest scientific foundation. At present, the risk-assessment procedures are distorted by a myriad of adjustment factors. Some of these adjustments are part of the assessment process, as scientists play the role of policy makers by inflating the risk assessments where scientific evidence is unclear. As a result, society might pay excessive attention to small risks that are not well understood, while it is comparatively lax toward greater but better understood risks.

This phenomenon is exacerbated under the provisions of the state labeling laws, which expand the scientific risk-assessment process. They multiply the risk levels by factors of 100 or 1,000, for example, for "conservatism." But incorporating biases into the scientific basis for the hazard-warnings program is in no sense conservative. This government-mandated misrepresentation means that we are lying to ourselves about the true levels of risk being posed. If we want the risk-communication policy to inform consumer choice in an honest manner that will promote more rational decision making, we must ensure that the scientific basis of this policy is honest as well.[1]

The second major change needed for the current Proposition 65 type of approach concerns the inappropriateness of tying the warnings system to the cigarette example. The risk levels involved are quite different from those of cigarettes or many other commonly labeled risks, such as those posed by household chemicals. We want the warnings system to reflect the particular risk accurately.

Two components of the warning are most instrumental. The wording is clearly of consequence, as we want it to suggest the risk level involved. And the mode of the warning is influential. The mere act of stamping a product as hazardous with an on-product label conveys a particularly high level of risk and earmarks the product as being relatively hazardous, irrespective of the wording of the label. The mode of warning selected consequently should be adjusted to reflect the level of the risk.

A useful starting-point for a policy approach would be a differentiated warnings system, such as a two-tiered one. The first tier could treat low levels of risk, of concern to particularly sensitive groups in society but unlikely to influence most consumers' deci-

---

[1]A. Nichols and R. J. Zeckhauser, "The Perils of Prudence: How Conservative Risk Assessments Distort Regulation," *Regulation*, vol. 10 (1986), pp. 11–24.

sions. Risks at the Proposition 65 threshold that would influence consumers' willingness to pay for a product by a penny per week are typical of such minimal-risk levels. A product at this level could carry a warning, but not on the product. Instead, a less obtrusive labeling system could communicate the presence of a potential hazard and the level of the risk. A reference binder could be made available at stores, for example. It could be analogous to the material safety data sheets currently used under OSHA regulations for hazard communication. Another possibility would be to publish an annual guide that provided a list of such low-risk products, not unlike the *Consumer Reports* annual buyers' guide. A low-cost paperback book would make information available to consumers in an easily referenced form.

Because of the low-cost nature of the disclosure, the scope of the classes of risk included could be broad as well. In addition to carcinogenic and reproductive hazards, for example, a list of artificial ingredients to which some consumers might have a sensitivity could be included.

The next tier of the system could consist of a more visible warning, in the form of an on-product label. An alternative could be a point-of-purchase display, but in-store approaches are not economically feasible and so are unlikely to be adopted.

The wording of this warning could differ from that now proposed in the various states. It could convey the true risk level posed, rather than a lifetime risk of 1/10.

A key policy issue is to determine the cutoff between products receiving the on-product warning and products receiving the first-tier warning. Making such a judgment depends largely on the distribution of product risks and the concentration of products in risk groups.

Notwithstanding the proliferation of the state warnings policies, we have as yet no meaningful assessment of the distribution of risks posed by food, drugs, and cosmetics. Constructing a risk-warnings system in the absence of such knowledge is similar to developing a grading system for eggs without knowing the distribution of sizes. Until we know the sizes of eggs, we cannot decide which ones should be labeled as jumbo, extra-large, large, or medium. We have to ascertain the distribution of the risks posed by these products before we can implement a pertinent tiered warnings system.

Once this distribution is known, the hazard-warning language and the mode of risk communication should be pretested before it is implemented. In various studies my colleagues and I have done for EPA, we have found it is difficult to predict the impact of warnings without ascertaining the consumer's response. The optimal approach is not to huddle a group of congressional staffers together over the weekend to draft the warnings language. This has often been the basis for government policy, as we have in effect run our warnings experiments on a national basis.

We can do much better than this narrow, legalistic approach by formulating alternative warning language and modes of presentation, by pretesting approaches on consumers, and by ascertaining whether the risks being communicated are commensurate with those posed by products. Recognition of the need for such pretesting would reflect an understanding of the complex cognitive processes that affect the efficacy of warnings. Most important, use of the pretesting option would recognize the critical role consumers play in this process. Consumer reaction and a knowledgeable response to the warning is a prerequisite for a successful warnings effort. A warnings program cannot treat the consumer response as an afterthought, but must instead integrate this response into the design of the risk-communication system.

Such a warnings approach promises to remedy whatever informational inadequacies are present yet not to distort the risky consumption decisions we hope to inform. Moreover, by adopting a federal approach that establishes a uniform and meaningful national warnings vocabulary, we can eliminate the unnecessary economic costs associated with Proposition 65 and related measures. The state warnings programs have served a constructive purpose by indicating a potentially fruitful area for federal involvement. The task now is to implement such a national strategy.

The federal government can ensure that any risk-communication policy is consistent with a broad array of other hazard-communication efforts. The federal government is better suited than the states to develop the scientific basis for ascertaining which products merit warnings and which do not. Responsibility for the safety of food, drugs, cosmetics, and medical devices should be a federal responsibility.

Safe Drinking Water and Toxic Enforcement Act of 1986

Chemicals Known to the State of California to Cause Cancer

A-alpha-C(2-Amino-9H-pyri-dol[2,3-b]indole)
Acetaldehyde
Acetamide
Acetochlor
2-Acetylaminofluorene
Acifluorfen
Acrylamide
Acrylonitrile
Actinomycin D
Adriamycin (Doxorubicin hydro-chloride)
AF-2;[2-(2-furyl)-3-(5-nitro-2-furyl)]acrylamide
Aflatoxins
Alachlor
Alcoholic beverages, when associated with alcohol abuse
Aldrin
Allyl chloride
2-Aminoanthraquinone
p-Aminoazotoluene
ortho-Aminoazotoluene

4-Aminobiphenyl(4-aminodi-phenyl)
3-Amino-9-ethylcarbazole hydro-chloride
1-Amino-2-methylanthraquinone
2-Amino-5-(5-nitro-2 furyl)-1,3,4-thiadiazole
Amitrole
Analgesic mixtures containing phenacetin
Aniline
ortho-Anisidine
ortho-Anisidine hydrochloride
Antimony oxide (Antimony triox-ide)
Aramite
Arsenic (inorganic arsenic com-pounds)
Asbestos
Auramine
Azaserine
Azathioprine
Azobenzene
Benz[a]anthracene

75

Benzene
Benzidine [and its salts]
Benzo[b]fluoranthene
Benzo[j]fluoranthene
Benzo[k]fluoranthene
Benzofuran
Benzo[a]pyrene
Benzotrichloride
Benzyl chloride
Benzyl violet 4B
Beryllium and beryllium compounds
Betel quid with tobacco
Bis(2-chloroethyl)-2-naphthylamine (Chlornapazine)
Bischloroethyl nitrosourea (BCNU) (Carmustine)
Bis(chloromethyl) ether
Bitumens, extracts of steam-refined and air refined
Bracken fern
Bromodichloromethane
Bromoform
1,3-Futadiene
1,4-Butanediol dimethanesulfonate (Busulfan)
Butylated hydroxyanisole
beta-Butyrolactone
Cadmium and cadmium compounds
Captafol
Captan
Carbon tetrachloride
Carbon-black extracts
Ceramic fibers (airborne particles of respirable size)
Certain combined chemotherapy for lymphomas
Chlorambucil
Chloramphenicol

Chlordane
Chlordecone (Kepone)
Chlordimeform
Chlorenic acid
Chlorinated paraffins (Average chain length, C12; approximately 60 percent chlorine by weight)
Chlorodibromomethane
Chloroethane (Ethyl chloride)
1-(2-Chloroethyl)-3-cyclohexyl-1-nitrosourea (CCNU) (Lomustine)
1-(2-Chloroethyl)-3-(4-methylcyclohexyl)-nitrosourea (Methyl-CCNU)
Chloroform
Chloromethyl methyl ether (technical grade)
3-Chloro-2-methylpropene
4-Chloro-ortho-phenylenediamine
p-Chloro-o-toluidine
Chlorothalonil
Chromium (hexavalent compounds)
Chrysene
C.I. Basic Red 9 monohydrochloride
Cinnamyl anthranilate
Cisplatin
Citrus Red No. 2
Coke oven emissions
Conjugated estrogens
Creosotes
para-Cresidine
Cupferron
Cycasin
Cyclophosphamide (anhydrous)
Cyclophosphamide (hydrated)
D&C Orange No. 17

D&C Red No. 8
D&C Red No. 9
D&C Red No. 19
Dacarbazine
Daminozide
Daunomycin
DDD (Dichlorodiphenyldichloroethane)
DDE (Dichlorodiphenyldichloroethylane)
DDT (Dichlorodiphenyltrichloroethane)
DDVP (Dichorvos)
N,N'-Diacetylbenzidine
2,4-Diaminoanisole
2,4-Diaminoanisole sulfate
4,4'-Diaminodiphenyl ether (4,4'-Oxydianiline)
2,4-Diaminotoluene
Diaminotoluene (mixed)
Dibenz[a,h]acridine
Dibenz[a,j]acridine
Dibenz[a,h]anthracene
7H-Dibenzo[c,g]carbazole
Dibenzo[a,e]pyrene
Dibenzo[a,h]pyrene
Dibenzo[a,i]pyrene
Dibenzo[a,l]pyrene
1,2-Dibromo-3-chloropropane (DBCP)
p-Dichlorobenzene
3,3'-Dichlorobenzidine
1,4-Dichloro-2-butene
3,3'-Dichloro-4,4'-diaminodiphenyl ether
1,1-Dichloroethane
Dichloromethane (Methylene chloride)
1,2-Dichloropropane
1,3-Dichloropropene

Dieldrin
Dienestrol
Diepoxybutane
Diesel engine exhaust
Di(2-ethylhexyl)phthalate
1,2-Diethylhydrazine
Diethyl sulfate
Diethylstillbestrol
Diglycidyl resorcinol ether (DGRE)
Dihydrosafrole
3-3'-Dimethoxybenzidine dihydrochloride (ortho-Dianisidine dihydrochloride)
Dimethyl sulfate
4-Dimethylaminoazobenzene
trans-2-[(Dimethylamino) methylamino]-5-[2-(5-nitro-2-furyl)vinyl]-1,3,4-oxadiazole
7,12-Dimethylbenz(a)anthracene
3,3'-Dimethylbenzidine (ortho-Tolidine)
Dimethylcarbamoyl chloride
1,1-Dimethylhydrazine
1,2-Dimethylhydrazine
Dimethylvinylchloride
1,6-Dinitropyrene
1,8-Dinitropyrene
2,4-Dinitrotoluene
1,4-Dioxane
Diphenylhydantoin (Phenytoin)
Diphenylhydantoin (Phenytoin), sodium salt
Direct Black 38 (technical grade)
Direct Blue 6 (technical grade)
Direct Brown 95 (technical grade)
Disperse Blue 1
Epichlorohydrin
Erionite
Estradiol 17β

Estrone
Ethinylestradiol
Ethyl acrylate
Ethyl methanesulfonate
Ethyl-4,4'-dichlorobenzilate
Ethylene dibromide
Ethylene dichloride (1,2-Dichloroethane)
Ethylene oxide
Ethylene thriourea
Ethyleneimine
Folpet
Formaldehyde (gas)
2-(2-Formylhydrazino)-4-(5-nitro-2-furyl)thiazole
Furazolidone
Furmecyclox
Gasoline engine exhaust (condensates/extracts)
Glasswool fibers (airborne particles of respirable size)
Glu-P-1(2-Amino-6-methyldipyridol[1,2-a:3',2'-d]imidazole)
Glu-P-2(2-Aminodipyrido[1,2-a:3',2'-d]imidazole)
Glycidaldehyde
Glycidol
Griseofulvin
Gyromitrin (Acetaldehyde methylformylhydrazone)
HC Blue 1
Heptachlor
Heptachlor epoxide
Hexachlorobenzene
Hexachlorocyclohexane (technical grade)
Hexachlorodibenzodioxin
Hexachloroethane
Hexamethylphosphoramide
Hydrazine
Hydrazine sulfate

Hydrazobenzene (1,2-Diphenylhydrazine)
Indeno[1,2,3-cd]pyrene
IQ(2-Amino-3-methylimidazo[4,5-f]quinoline)
Iron dextran complex
Isosafrole
Lactofen
Lasiocarpine
Lead acetate
Lead phosphate
Lead subacetate
Lindane and other hexachlorocyclohexane isomers
Mancozeb
Maneb
Me-A-alpha-C(2-Amino-3-methyl-9H-pyrido[2,3-b]indole)
Medroxyprogesterone acetate
Melphalan
Merphalan
Mestranol
8-Methoxypsoralen with ultraviolet A therapy
5-Methoxypsoralen with ultraviolet A therapy
2-Methylaziridine (Propyleneimine)
Methylazoxymethanol
Methylazoxymethanol acetate
3-Methylcholanthrene
5-Methylchrysene
4,4'-Methylene bis(2-chloroaniline)
4,4'-Methylene bis(N,N-dimethyl)benzenamine
4,4'-Methylene bis(2-methylaniline)
4,4'-Methylenedianiline
4,4'-Methylenedianiline dihydrochloride

Methyl iodide

Methyl methanesulfonate

2-Methyl-1-nitroanthraquinone (of uncertain purity)

N-Methyl-N'-nitro-N-nitrosoguanidine

N-Methylacrylamide

Methylthiouracil

Metiram

Metronidazole

Michler's ketone

Mirex

Mitomycin C

Monocrotaline

5-(Morpholinomethyl)-3-[(5-nitrofurfurylidene)-amino]-2-oxaloidinone

Mustard Gas

Nafenopin

1-Naphthylamine

2-Naphthylamine

Nickel and certain nickel compounds

Nickel carbonyl

Nickel refinery dust from the pyrometallurgical process

Nickel subsulfide

Niridazole

Nitrilotriacetic acid

Nitrilotriacetic acid, trisodium salt monohydrate

5-Nitroacenaphthene

5-Nitro-o-anisidine

4-Nitrobiphenyl

6-Nitrochrysene

Nitrofen (technical grade)

2-Nitrofluorene

1-[(5-Nitrofurfurylidene)-amino]-2-imidazolidinone

N-[4-(5-Nitro-2-furyl)-2-thiazolyl]acetamide

Nitrogen mustard [Mechlorethamine]

Nitrogen mustard hydrochloride (Mechlorethamine hydrochloride)

Nitrogen mustard N-oxide

Nitrogen mustard N-oxide hydrochloride

2-Nitropropane

1-Nitropyrene

4-Nitropyrene

N-Nitrodosi-n-butylamine

N-Nitrosodiethanolamine

N-Nitrosodiethylamine

N-Nitrosodimethylamine

p-Nitrosodiphenylamine

N-Nitrosodiphenylamine

N-Nitrosodi-n-propylamine

N-Nitroso-N-ethylurea

3-(N-Nitrosomethylamino)propionitrile

4-(N-Nitrosomethylamino)-1-(3-pyridyl)-1-butanone

N-Nitrosomethylethylamine

N-Nitroso-N-methylurea

N-Nitroso-N-methylurethane

N-Nitrosomethylvinylamine

N-Nitrosomorpholine

N-Nitrosonornicotine

N-Nitrosopiperidine

N-Nitrososarcosine

Norethisterone (Norethindrone)

Ochratoxin A

Oil Orange SS

Oral contraceptives, combined

Oral contraceptives, sequential

Oxadazon

Oxymetholone

Panfuran S

Pentachlorophenol

Phenacetin

Phenazopyridine
Phenazopyridine hydrochloride
Phenesterin
Phenobarbital
Phenoxybenzamine
Phenoxybenzamine hydrochloride
Phenyl glycidyl ether
o-Phenylphenate, sodium
Polybrominated biphenyls
Polychlorinated biphenyls
Polychlorinated biphenyls (containing 60 or more percent chlorine by molecular weight)
Polygeenan
Ponceau MX
Ponceau 3R
Potassium bromate
Procarbazine
Procarbazine hydrochloride
Progesterone
1,3-Propane sultone
beta-Propiolactone
Propylene oxide
Propylthiouracil
Radionuclides
Reserpine
Residual (heavy) fuel oils
Saccharin
Saccharin, sodium
Safrole
Selenium sulfide
Shale-oils
Silica, crystalline (airborne particles of respirable size)
Soots, tars, and mineral oils (untreated and mildly treated oils and used engine oils)
Sterigmatocystin
Streptozotocin
Styrene oxide
Sulfallate

Talc containing asbestiform fibers
Testosterone and its esters
2,3,7,8-Tetrachlorodibenzo-para-dioxin (TCDD)
1,1,2,2-Tetrachloroethane
Tetranitromethane
Thioacetamide
Thiourea
Thorium dioxide
Tobacco, oral use of smokeless products
Tobacco smoke
Toluene diisocyanate
ortho-Toluidine hydrochloride
para-Toluidine
Toxaphene (Polychlorinated camphenes)
Treosulfan
2,4,6-Trichlorophenol
Trichloroethylene
Tris(aziridinyl)-para-benzoquinone (Triaziquone)
Tris(1-aziridinyl)phosphine sulfide (Thiotepa)
Tris(2,3-dibromopropyl)phosphate
Trp-P-1(Tryptophan-P-1)
Trp-P-2(Tryptophan-P-2)
Trypan blue (commercial grade)
Unleaded gasoline (wholly vaporized)
Uracil mustard
Urethane (Ethyl carbamate)
Vinyl bromide
Vinyl chloride
4-Vinyl-1-cyclohexene diepoxide (Vinyl cyclohexene dioxide)
Vinyl trichloride (1,1-2-Trichloroethane)
2,6-Xylidene(2,6-Dimethylaniline)
Zineb

Chemicals Known to the State to Cause Reproductive Toxicity

Developmental Toxicity

Acetohydroxamic acid
All-trans retinoic acid
Alprazolam
Amikacin sulfate
Aminoglutethimide
Aminopterin
Aspirin[1]
Benomyl
Benzphetamine hydrochloride
Bischloroethyl nitrosourea (BCNU) (Carmustine)
Bromoxynil
1,4-Butanediol dimethylsulfonate (Busulfan)
Carbon disulfide
Carbon monoxide
Carboplatin
Chenodiol
Chlorcyclizine hydrochloride
Chlorambucil
Chlordecone (Kepone)
1-(2-Chloroethyl)-3-cyclohexyl-1-nitrosourea (CCNU) (Lomustine)
Clomiphene citrate
Cocaine
Conjugated estrogens
Cyanazine
Cycloheximide
Cyclophosphamide (anhydrous)
Cyclophosphamide (hydrated)
Cyhexatin
Cytarabine
Danazol
Daunorubicin hydrochloride

Diethylstillbestrol (DES)
Dinocap
Dinoseb
Diphenylhydantoin (Phenytoin)
Doxycycline
Ergotamine tartrate
Ethyl alcohol in alcoholic beverages
Ethylene glycol monoethyl ether
Ethylene glycol monomethyl ether
Etoposide
Etretinate
Fluoruouracil
Fluoxymeserone
Flutamide
Halazepam
Hexachlorobenzene
Ifosfamide
Iodine-131
Isotretinoin
Lead
Lithium carbonate
Lithium citrate
Lorazepam
Medroxyprogesterone acetate
Megestrol acetate
Melphalan
Menotropins
Mercaptopurine
Mercury and mercury compounds
Methacycline hydrochloride
Methimazole
Methotrexate
Methotrexate sodium

[1]It is especially important not to use aspirin during the last three months of pregnancy, unless specifically directed to do so by a physician, because it may cause problems in the unborn child or complications during delivery.

Methyl mercury
Methyltestosterone
Midazolam hydrochloride
Misoprostol
Mitroxantrone hydrochloride
Nafarelin acetate
Netilmicin sulfate
Nicotine
Nitrogen mustard (Mechlorethamine)
Nitrogen mustard hydrochloride (Mechlorethamine hydrochloride)
Norethisterone (Norethindrone)
Norethisterone (Norethindrone)/ Ethinyl estradiol
Norethisterone (Norethindrone)/ Mestranol
Norgestrel
Oxytetracycline
Paramethadione
Penicillamine
Pentobarbital sodium
Phenacemide
Pipobroman
Plicamycin
Polychlorinated biphenyls

Procarbazine hydrochloride
Propylthiouracil
Retinol/retinyl esters, when in daily dosages in excess of 10,000 IU, or 3,000 retinol equivalents[2]
Ribavirin
Streptomycin sulfate
Tamoxifen citrate
Temazepam
Testosterone enanthate
2,3,7,8-Tetrachlorodibenzo-para-dioxin (TCDD)
Tetracycline hydrochloride
Thalidomide
Thioguanine
Tobacco smoke (primary)
Tobramycin sulfate
Toluene
Triazolam
Trilostane
Trimethalone
Urofollitropin
Valproate
Vinblastine sulfate
Vincristine sulfate
Warfarin

Female Reproductive Toxicity

Aminopterin
Anabolic steroids
Aspirin[3]
Carbon disulfide
Cocaine

Cyclophosphamide (anhydrous)
Cyclophosphamide (hydrated)
Ethylene oxide
Lead
Tobacco smoke (primary)

---

[2]Retinol/retinyl esters are required and essential for maintenance of normal reproductive function. The recommended daily level during pregnancy is 8,000 IU.

[3]It is especially important not to use aspirin during the last three months of pregnancy, unless specifically directed to do so by a physician, because it may cause problems in the unborn child or complications during delivery.

Male Reproductive Toxicity

Anabolic steroids
Benomyl
Carbon disulfide
Cyclophosphamide (anhydrous)
Cyclophosphamide (hydrated)
1,2-Dibromo-3-chloropropane
  (DBCP)
m-Dinitrobenzene

o-Dinitrobenzene
p-Dinitrobenzene
Dinoseb
Ethylene glycol monoethyl ether
Ethylene glycol monomethyl ether
Lead
Nitrofurantoin
Tobacco smoke (primary)

Sam Peltzman
Sears Roebuck Professor of Economics
and Financial Services
University of Chicago
Graduate School of Business

Nelson W. Polsby
Professor of Political Science
University of California at Berkeley

Murray L. Weidenbaum
Mallinckrodt Distinguished
University Professor
Washington University

Research Staff

Leon Aron
Resident Scholar

Claude E. Barfield
Resident Scholar; Director, Science
and Technology Policy Studies

Walter Berns
Adjunct Scholar

Douglas J. Besharov
Resident Scholar

Jagdish Bhagwati
Visiting Scholar

Robert H. Bork
John M. Olin Scholar in Legal Studies

Dinesh D'Souza
John M. Olin Research Fellow

Nicholas N. Eberstadt
Visiting Scholar

Mark Falcoff
Resident Scholar

Gerald R. Ford
Distinguished Fellow

Murray F. Foss
Visiting Scholar

Suzanne Garment
Resident Scholar

Patrick Glynn
Resident Scholar

Robert A. Goldwin
Resident Scholar

Gottfried Haberler
Resident Scholar

Robert W. Hahn
Resident Scholar

Robert B. Helms
Resident Scholar

Karlyn H. Keene
Resident Fellow; Editor,
The American Enterprise

Jeane J. Kirkpatrick
Senior Fellow; Director, Foreign and
Defense Policy Studies

Marvin H. Kosters
Resident Scholar; Director,
Economic Policy Studies

Irving Kristol
John M. Olin Distinguished Fellow

Michael A. Ledeen
Resident Scholar

Susan Lee
DeWitt Wallace–Reader's Digest
Fellow in Communications
in a Free Society

Robert A. Licht
Resident Scholar; Director,
Constitution Project

Chong-Pin Lin
Resident Scholar; Associate Director,
China Studies Program

John H. Makin
Resident Scholar; Director, Fiscal
Policy Studies

Allan H. Meltzer
Visiting Scholar

Joshua Muravchik
Resident Scholar

Charles Murray
Bradley Fellow

Michael Novak
George F. Jewett Scholar in Religion,
Philosophy, and Public Policy;
Director, Social and
Political Studies

Norman J. Ornstein
Resident Scholar

Richard N. Perle
Resident Fellow

Thomas W. Robinson
Resident Scholar: Director, China
Studies Program

William Schneider
Resident Fellow

Bill Shew
Visiting Scholar

J. Gregory Sidak
Resident Scholar

Herbert Stein
Senior Fellow

Irwin M. Stelzer
Resident Scholar; Director, Regulatory
Policy Studies

Edward Styles
Director of Publications

W. Allen Wallis
Resident Scholar

Ben J. Wattenberg
Senior Fellow

Carolyn L. Weaver
Resident Scholar; Director, Social
Security and Pension Studies